ALICE NSABIMANA

AFTER ALL WAS LOST

The Resilience of a Rwandan Family Orphaned on April 6, 1994
when the Rwandan President's Plane was Shot Down

Translated from the French by
Maurice Nsabimana

Baraka
Books

Montréal

When the Chief of Staff of Rwanda's Army was assassinated, after the invasion of the country, civil war and then
genocide, his widow and their six children found ways to
overcome the rupture of their family—and their country.
This is their story.

Alice Nsabimana

ISBN 978-1-77186-313-1 pbk; 978-1-77186-326-1 epub; 978-1-77186-327-8 pdf

Cover and Book Design by Folio infographie
Editing and proofreading: Robin Philpot, Blossom Thom

Legal Deposit, 3rd quarter 2023
Bibliothèque et Archives nationales du Québec
Library and Archives Canada

Published by Baraka Books of Montreal

Printed and bound in Quebec

Trade Distribution & Returns
Canada – UTP Distribution: UTPdistribution.com

United States
Independent Publishers Group: IPGbook.com

Contents

Preface

By Mr. Johan Swinnen, Belgian Ambassador to Rwanda between 1990 and 1994.

Twenty-seven years after the Rwandan tragedy, we are still searching for the whole truth behind this horrific and tragic experience.

The story of the genocide, its prelude, its unfolding, and its outcome is rarely told in all aspects. Too often, history is incomplete. At worst, the story is marred by polarizing simplifications, biases, ambiguities, one-sided presentations, or outright lies.

Indeed, the search for truth is hampered by unjust insinuations and accusations of revisionism or negationism. However, truth seekers do not give up. On the contrary, they know well the necessity and liberating impact of taking a strong stand against crippling political correctness, oppressive single-mindedness, and one-sided, fabricated propaganda.

Alice Nsabimana shows courage and diligence in recounting the story of her family, steeped in nostalgic memories of carefree youth, full of dreams and harmony, but shaken by the painful degradation of a process that was supposed to lead to peace and democracy but which, in the end, goes wrong and ends in a terrible and appalling genocide.

2 AFTER ALL WAS LOST

Her father, Major General Déogratias Nsabimana, Chief of Staff of the Rwandan army, perished with the president in the April 6, 1994, attack against the presidential Falcon.

The description of the dismembered remains of her father is particularly moving and poignant. But the immense grief of the family does not turn into despair and defeatism. In Alice's serene and strong attitude, a young girl barely seventeen, and that of her mother and her family, I recognize the dignity and resilience of many Rwandan families with whom I kept in touch after the genocide or whom I have come to know.

Alice's testimony intrigued me because I knew her father personally. In my book *Rwanda, My Story*, where I recount my experience as a Belgian ambassador in Kigali from August 1990 until the start of the genocide in April 1994, I welcome his appointment as Chief of Staff of the Rwandan army at the end of June 1992. This appointment coincided with the beginning of the peace negotiations in Arusha and had, in my opinion, a beneficial impact on the morale of the military troops.

The compromises negotiated in Arusha on sharing political and military power, with substantial concessions made on the government's side, could not shake the general's confidence in the peace process. Alice is impressed by his belief in peace and reconciliation, the only way to achieve *"Rwanda's renewal."* But unfortunately, this hope is shattered when the democratization process in neighboring Burundi receives a fatal blow with the assassination of President Ndadaye.

I remember well the Chief of Staff's disenchantment when he said to me: *"Arusha is overwhelmed. Power sharing must take into account the new political configuration following the coup in Burundi. From now on, the ethnic connotation is in full swing."* He thus expressed a widespread fear. Even in moderate circles, more and more voices were being raised to fear what was called the imminent return of the old domination.

I also have very vivid memories of the meeting between President Habyarimana, Colonel Luc Marchal, and myself, which General Nsabimana organized at his residence in Ndera in February 1994, a few weeks before the dramatic explosion. The President and his Chief of Staff then told us how attached they were to the positive development of the peace process and to the important role that the Belgians should play in this context. A few days later, General Nsabimana visited the Belgian detachment of the United Nations Assistance Mission for Rwanda (UNAMIR). Young Alice must no doubt have kept an eye on these confabulations from a distance!

Alice's story and my memories show that Déogratias Nsabimana was driven by "hopes punctuated by worries" and the realization that "the only viable option was the unity of Rwandans."

The testimony of the Nsabimana siblings, and Alice in particular, is remarkable for its positive and grateful tone. Of course, there is a lot of nostalgia and sadness, but she has no bitterness towards her homeland. No resentment, no hatred. Alice also understood very well that their father carried a message which still has particular value today and which she formulated as follows:

> Our father taught us never to judge people by their ethnicity, and by extension their race, their origin, their skin color, their religion.

In my view, this account also makes an enriching contribution to the complex history of the genocide. A country that creates opportunities for civic openness, bereavement, and truth-seeking initiatives increases its chances of accepting the trauma of the past and embarking on a lasting path of sustainable reconciliation and development. Alice, Déogratias' daughter, has taken this path.

Dedication

This book is dedicated to our mother, Athanasie Uwimana, who did not just give us life. She has loved us unconditionally since our childhood; she has been our rock since the death of our father.

She was born in 1951 in Gisenyi, a prefecture located in the north of Rwanda. She married in 1971 and supported our father, following him in his various assignments abroad. She is our "Minister of the Interior," the strong hand who has always managed the house. When we fled Rwanda in April 1994, she was only forty-three. As the adults and parents we are now, we can only admire her more today. Overnight, she went from wife and respected businesswoman with a huge residence and staff to widowed, solo mom of six. Yet, she didn't hesitate to roll up her sleeves and start over again to give us a home.

She played the role of father and mother, counselor and therapist, managing to bring food, and making every effort to ensure that each of us had an education. She stayed strong and taught us to think positively, be persistent, and love our neighbors. She is undeniably a great lady, modern, independent, and ahead of her time. When our father died, she had to carry us one by one, using all her strength and courage to give us the best of herself while allowing us to build ourselves up as men and women. It allowed us to be free in our choices. The one word she never wanted to hear from us, and she still doesn't, is "impossible." According to her, if we think very hard about it and visualize the object of our desire, we reach it. Anything is possible.

In 2016, exactly on October 3, we learned with horror that Mom had cancer. The last time she went to the hospital was to give birth to our younger brother in 1985! Apart from that, we never saw her sick or complaining of any ailment, except for her occasional ingrown nails! So, we thought she was superhuman, almost invincible. First seized by fear, we united around her to breathe into her all the positive waves possible. Mom then said that if Alexander, her grandson, and son of our older brother, had survived liver cancer a few years ago when he was only two years old, she could do it too. She fought hard, enduring with dignity and without ever complaining about the pain inflicted by radiotherapy and chemotherapy. By the grace of God and a wonderful medical team that we thank so much, she got out of it, and we pray that she can still live long and happy years with all of us.

She is now the grandmother of sixteen grandchildren whom she has carried in turn, according to the Rwandan tradition of *Guheka,* which is transmitted from generation to generation and consists of carrying her child on her back from early childhood, creating a mother-child closeness and allowing the mother to go about her business while watching over her baby.

Based on the notion that "what does not kill us makes us stronger," we have all chosen to rebuild ourselves from our traumas and transmit our values of peace and love around us. We also dedicate this book to our children: Maxime, Hilarion, Eloha, Mia, Kessya, Sofia, Amani, Alexander,

Keona, Timothy, Raphaël, Gabriel, Tessa, Luna, Malaïka, and Dea.

Finally, this book is dedicated to all Rwandans who will recognize themselves in this story.

Kiyovu, April 6, 1994, around 8:30 p.m.

It's the Easter holidays. We sit comfortably in the living room to watch *The Sound of Music,* a great classic and one of our favorite films. We just have time to see the credits scrolling when a huge explosion occurs, followed by a second explosion a few seconds later. This time, it has nothing to do with the sounds of Kalashnikovs that we sometimes hear and have learned to distinguish. We rush to the terrace and see a yellow-orange light shining in the distance. Our bodyguards rush up and order us to go back inside. The phones start ringing all over the place: "Where is General Nsabimana? This is an emergency! It's chaos."

After about twenty interminable and emotionally unbearable minutes, after repeating again and again the same answer to everybody who asks—"No, Dad hasn't come home yet"—and after hearing that an attack had taken place but that there were two planes, the violent and unequivocal statement pierces us with full force: "All the occupants who boarded the presidential Falcon are dead. We are busy collecting the body parts scattered around the presidential residence."

It is unimaginable that he would leave now when he seemed so close to the goal. He told us that peace was, perhaps, on the verge of finally seeing the light of day. . . . And yet, everything changed on that evening of April 6, for many thousands of people, and for us.

Introduction

In Rwanda, many names refer to God as *Imana*. Our surname **Nsabimana** means "I pray to God." Our parents wanted to give each of us other Catholic first names, but also Rwandan ones, which had a very special meaning in their eyes or were given in memory of our ancestors.

My name is **Alice**. I was born in 1977. I have two brothers and three sisters and the privilege of being the third Nsabimana sibling.

On April 12, 1994, amid chaos, a force that I did not think I had pushed me to call Dad's military adviser, who had us evacuated from Kigali. From that day on, I promised myself that when the time came, when I had made peace with my past, I would take my courage in both hands and tell my family history. And, at the same time, I would pay tribute to all those heroes, starting with Dad, who perished in the name of their country; to those countless innocent lives and to those who dared to save lives, at the risk of their own.

I have always been called Miss Organization, a quality I inherited from Dad. However, as an adult, I realized that positive and negative events tend to converge on me because of my middle position. In my work, I also discovered that I had the ability to listen, to help others, and to absorb their concerns with the satisfaction that it would help them overcome their problems. This is how I decided on my career; I wanted to train in mediation, with the ambition of possibly contributing to lasting and peaceful relations among Rwandans.

To facilitate the reading of this book, it will be my voice that will carry our story by striving to report faithfully the experience of each of my brothers and sisters, whom I first present to you briefly.

Maurice, our eldest, was born in 1972. Two words to define Maurice would be "living encyclopedia." As far back as I can remember, Maurice always had excellent marks at school and, later, a remarkable general culture. Laid back, he does everything slowly, and that can be irritating at times, but there's a lot of wisdom in everything he says and does. After Dad's death, as is the custom in Rwanda and many other African cultures, Maurice inherited the role of head of the family. He became our protective figure, ensuring that each of us found an emotional balance. Maurice always pushes us to learn by reading. What's more, each problem corresponds to a book according to him. And some libraries pale in comparison to his superb collection.

The tragedy we experienced transformed him and aroused in him the desire to establish inasmuch as possible a lasting peace in the Rwandan, African, or worldwide context. As a result, his most pronounced character trait is levelheadedness. Over time, he learned to let go of "unimportant" things and to focus on how he could make the world around him better by how he was, thought, and acted.

Denise was born in 1974. She is our silent strength. As a teenager (and even as an adult), she remained true to herself: upright and persevering. Her strong point is her ability to listen, whether in private or at work (it is not by chance that she flourishes in human resources).

She left Rwanda at eighteen to pursue her higher education in Belgium. Unfortunately, the tragedy of 1994 struck without her having the opportunity to return to Rwanda. This one-way trip, therefore, particularly traumatized her.

Twenty years later, she took a big step by treading the red earth of Rwanda's Thousand Hills to submit to the extremely painful exercise of *Kwibuka* or remembering and soaking up the smells of the red earth of the land of a Thousand Hills.

Yvonne is our Miss Peace & Love. She was born in 1981. She is very spiritual and ready to bend over backwards to help; she is goodness incarnate. As a child, she was a "tomboy." Her favorite activity was climbing trees and playing Ninjas with her younger siblings and friends. Sociable and resourceful, she knew our neighborhood by heart. Enterprising, she leaves her mark on each city she passes through, either by setting up a dance school or a cultural association. Just as Dad served his country, having admittedly chosen a dangerous profession, she chose to serve the people of her host country. She is a teacher, and this profession has become a second nature because she has this gift of transmitting knowledge naturally and patiently. Sharing the life of each of her students is an honor for her and gives her immense happiness.

Josiane, aka Jojo or Joe, is a true artist. She was born in 1983. As a baby, she was a child who spent her time walking around with her cuddly toy, always calm but ready to explode when necessary. A fashionista at heart, she has always had the art of combining materials. A born avant-gardist, she has a flair for unearthing improbable or banal pieces that transform such secondhand articles into luxury items.

Enterprising, persevering, and passionate, Josiane made her dream come true by creating her own clothing brand bearing her Rwandan name *Muhire*, which means luck.

Fabrice, our youngest sibling, was born in 1985. After four daughters, I think my parents ardently wished to have a boy, and their wish was fulfilled with his birth. Fabrice is the last of the "three musketeers," with Yvonne and Josiane. In Rwanda, he was the turbulent child, Mom's baby, whose clothes had to be changed three times a day. He and I didn't interact much until he grew up and became an adult. Today, Fabrice is our driving force. He is authentic and like a breed of bulldog, he never lets go and tells us straight from the hip what he thinks is right.

Time, perseverance, and all our fraternal love helped us to tell, in writing, part of our history. This book, which we wanted to be family-friendly, serves three goals.

First, it is for our children. Becoming adults and parents encouraged us to pass on our history to future generations. Our children are the mirror of what we were and have lived. They are naturally attracted by a part of their common culture that they have not yet had the opportunity to experience fully, which intrigues them more and more. These cousins, who have Rwandan, Belgian, American, Ghanaian, Cameroonian, Congolese, Salvadoran, Romanian, and Swiss blood flowing through their veins, have as a common denominator Rwanda, the "land of a thousand hills." Most have not yet had the chance to walk on our native land. They will never know their grandfather, unfortunately. That is why we want to pass on his legacy to them through the stories and anecdotes that marked certain chapters of his life.

Secondly, it is a duty of memory and a tribute to the one we consider our pillar. We wish to pay tribute to our father through our memories, through the testimonies of loved ones, and perpetuate his memory through his personal notes. Our memories of our father are those of a man who wanted peace for all Rwandans. He died in office while traveling on a mission of peace, a mission in which he firmly believed. After we left Rwanda in tragic circumstances, abandoning our father's body and leaving behind a large part of the family and, incidentally, all our belongings and memories, God gave us a chance to rebuild ourselves "elsewhere." Even though our lives and futures have changed from one minute to the next, we are alive and grateful. As time passes, we always support each other, talk, exchange, and spend time together to perpetuate the memory of Dad.

Finally, writing this book is like healing for us. Watching what is happening in the world, from accidents to natural disasters, from wars to pandemics, we are grateful to have been given a second chance. Certainly, there is a before and an after April 6, 1994. That date completely altered the course of our lives. Although no legal truth has yet been established on the exact circumstances of Dad's death and that of his fellow travelers, we have chosen the path of love to allow us to heal our wounds and continue to advance. We completely subscribe to this magnificent quote from Martin Luther King: "Hatred paralyzes life; love releases it. Hatred confuses life; love harmonizes it. Hatred darkens life; love illuminates it."

CHAPTER 1

The Life of the Nsabimana Family before the Death of the Patriarch

A definition of a patriarch in the Larousse dictionary is a "venerable old man, an elder, who is surrounded by numerous descendants." It may seem surprising to use this term to name someone who died only at the age of forty-nine. People of the older generation had so many responsibilities early on while they were so young that they already looked old through our children's eyes.

In traditional Rwandan culture, a man must take care of his family, especially if he manages to achieve a certain level of comfort in society. During his lifetime, Dad felt a duty to help as many people as possible grow with him. He wanted to give opportunities to those around him. I remember he always said that it was better to help someone by opening doors for them and letting them evolve than by giving them something to sustain themselves in the short term.

His life was short but filled with many accomplishments and achievements. Ultimately, he had the opportunity of bringing a stone to build his country as well as his large family, who considered him the patriarch.

Déogratias Nsabimana was born on August 23, 1945, in Nkuli, in the prefecture of Ruhengeri, located in the north of Rwanda. He was the only boy in the family and had four sisters. His father, Nicolas Ndalifite, and his mother, Marcianne Nyirambona, had eight children, three of whom died very young. The five remaining children were named Généreuse Hakuzimana, Julienne Kankindi, Dative Nkundabakura, Déogratias Nsabimana, and Esther Nirere.

Dad's father was a schoolteacher, and his family lacked nothing. His childhood was simple and happy. The traditional Northern dish, *impungure*, consisting of corn and beans, was often served at the table. Meat was then a rare commodity. Goat meat was not recommended for women (it was said that they risked growing facial hair if they ate it). In contrast, the consumption of lamb was strictly forbidden in the Ababanda clan to which Dad belonged.

He attended primary school in Rambura, in Gisenyi prefecture in northern Rwanda. When he was only eight, Dad nearly died of a serious illness. The village healer, who used traditional plants, then predicted that he was not going to leave so soon because he was going to have a glorious future that would have a great impact on people.

After attending secondary school at Musanze College, he chose to join the army, influenced by one of his cousins. At twenty-one, he entered the Rwandan Military Academy (Officers' School) in Kigali, where he graduated head of his class.

He met Mom at the wedding of his younger sister Esther in 1970. Another of his older sisters, Dative, lived in the neighboring province, Gisenyi, where Mom is from. Dad and Mom married a year later, then lived in the Rwandan capital Kigali for their first two years as a couple. Dad then worked as an aide-de-camp to the first Rwandan president, Grégoire Kayibanda.

At the beginning of 1972, after our brother Maurice was born, Dad obtained a scholarship to the Belgian Royal Military Academy in Brussels.

Dad therefore left Rwanda when Maurice was only a few months old and went ahead of his family to begin his studies and find family accommodation. A few months later, Mom and Maurice joined him.

1. The carefree period

We lived abroad during our childhood, which, in our opinion, greatly contributed to our openness to the world and its different cultures.

Belgium (from 1973 to 1980)

After Mom and Maurice arrived in Belgium, the family moved into an apartment in Schaerbeek at the beginning of 1973.

Later, once she found her bearings, Mom found a job as an administrative assistant at the Rwandan embassy in Brussels. She later left the job when the family grew with the birth of Denise in 1974.

Dad completed his training as a Command and General Staff Officer at the École de Guerre (Belgium's Royal Higher Institute for Defense, previously War College). He graduated with a "General Staff Brevet" (*Brevet d'état-major* or *BEM* in French) in 1975. He then began a diplomatic career.

That same year, he was appointed military attaché to the Rwandan embassy in Brussels, Belgium. As a result, the family moved into diplomatic quarters in

Watermael-Boitsfort. Maurice remembers a large garden where he loved to run. He describes his childhood then as happy and carefree. His most vivid memory is that there were always people at the residence. They ranged from Rwandans living in Brussels to dignitaries passing through during their mission in Belgium, or even people who stayed with us for a while when they came for long medical treatment, or even students before they found permanent accommodation. One of these guests taught Maurice to ride a bicycle, while another introduced him to archery in the garden. Maurice also remembers that our helper, who came from Rwanda, spent his time cooking.

He was a little boy then. A few years later, when he understood the context, he was also marked by the things happening around him that were clearly reserved for the adult world. Although most of the time there was only laughter, occasionally loud voices and rowdy debates could be heard coming from the living room. Dad and Mom often mediated for other Rwandan couples. Maurice remembers the case of a lady and her two children who had taken refuge at our home following a violent argument with her husband. There were also other children who had been sent to Europe following a stormy divorce in Rwanda and spent a few months with us before being placed in a foster family. This episode particularly marked Maurice because they would go and see the children in their new home where they seemed happy, except for the youngest who had suddenly become belligerent. The kids came to our home from time to time to spend the weekend.

At that time, Dad also drank too much sometimes, and this of course led to arguments with Mom.

Maurice remembers the day of April 6, 1977. That day, Dad came home very sad. His father had just died at the age of seventy following an illness. It was the first time that Maurice had seen him cry. Fate ordained that Dad would die on the same day seventeen years later, April 6, 1994.

Happy moments marked their daily lives. Almost every Saturday, Dad took the family to eat at one of his favorite restaurants, *Le Coucou* in Ixelles, in the Brussels region. One day, as they left the restaurant, they ran into a lady Mom had probably not seen for years. Immediately, they fell into each other's arms, crying. The last time they had seen each other was during troubled times in Rwanda in the late 1960s. Mom's family had then helped her friend's Tutsi family to flee, and, since then, they had lost touch. Nevertheless, they were so happy to see each other again, both alive. Mom introduced her friend Immaculée to Dad, telling him they were neighbors and friends in Gisenyi, and they had studied there together.

The trips, especially to Rwanda during the summer holidays, were exciting, filled with exotic and fascinating discoveries. Part of the stay took place in Kigali, the other between Nkuli and Karago, Dad and Mom's hometowns in the northwest of Rwanda. It was time to reconnect with the cousins.

Life with our grandparents was very simple. The only touch of modernity were the clothes they wore. For the rest, Maurice, who was still small, found it amusing to eat with his fingers by the light of a kerosene lamp. Like a good Rwandan father, Dad kept telling him that when he was little, he went to fetch water every day for his mother before walking several kilometers to school. Like Dad as a child, Maurice and the village children crossed large valleys to get to the well. He often came home soaked because he spilled most of the water on himself on the way back. He had a hard time carrying the bucket on his head. It was only after growing up and making regular visits that Maurice realized this was not a game but the daily life of his peers.

Denise also remembers the family home in Brussels, in Watermael-Boitsfort, nestled in a green district. She and Maurice spent a lot of time playing with the neighborhood kids. At the time, long before the media coverage of pedophilia cases, children were allowed to roam freely in the area. They were told never to go more than two blocks away. But breaking these rules had of course become so common that they thought they had mastered the streets of the small town by heart.

One day, they explored the neighborhood for hours, going deeper and deeper into the small alleys. They got lost until the police found them after noticing frightened-looking children. Maurice, who was six at the time, knew the family names of our parents and their nationality, which enabled the police, after a search, to bring them home safe and sound. They were just cold and scared. After thanking the police, Denise and Maurice were scolded, especially Maurice. Dad's most common punishment was to pull our ears as if to force them to listen better. On rare occasions like this, Maurice remembers seeing Dad's belt unroll from his waist in slow motion, like in movies, before it came down on him. A correction that came back to him every time he thought of venturing far and wide or when Denise wanted to go further than the authorized limits.

Music was always playing in the house. The melodies of Abba and Boney M still course through Denise's head. She also remembers the people who came to the house one after the other. Some came to spend a happy moment while others seemed to pour out their worries. Sometimes the arguments she heard behind the door when there were guests made her think that times were not that easy for them. Some lacked financial means, others lacked rest as they found themselves away from home with a new culture and a way of life to adopt ... But this suggests that our parents must have been *bon vivants* who loved people. That is what people have said about them.

As for me, I came into the world in 1977 and was barely three when we left Belgium. I obviously have no memory of my early childhood there. I was told I was a good little girl who liked observing everything around me. As the third sibling, with a three- and a five-year-old ahead of me, I had to find things to do and learn to be imaginative in play because I couldn't keep up with the older ones.

Libya (from 1980 to 1984)

When Dad was appointed military attaché to the Rwandan embassy in Tripoli, Libya, we all moved there in 1980.

Maurice's first memory is the intense heat that he felt as soon as the plane touched down at Tripoli airport and the air conditioning that did not work the first night spent in the house. This climate-related discomfort, unfortunately, continued for him. Very quickly, he began to develop repeated acute conjunctivitis accompanied by coughing, which led him to spend most of his time in the infirmary of the French school we attended.

Since diplomats were not encouraged to have their families treated there, Maurice was sent back to Belgium and diagnosed as "allergic to tropical climates." It wasn't until I questioned it fairly recently that I realized it wasn't a joke or a myth. Our parents had explained to us twice (in Libya in 1980 and a few years later in Rwanda in 1984) that Maurice could not stand hot climates, but at the time I found it so far-fetched ...

After a few weeks, Maurice returned to Tripoli with a variety of medications to alleviate his symptoms and improve his quality of life. But that didn't happen. He continued to have conjunctivitis regularly and found himself in the infirmary almost all the time when he was not bedridden at home. Every three months, he had to go to Belgium with Mom to do additional examinations to try to find other more effective remedies. He nonetheless finished his school year somehow. Finally, my parents decided to enroll him in a school in Belgium. Suffice it to say that his time in Tripoli was short and not the happiest for him.

In July 1981, Maurice traveled to Belgium with Mom, then six months pregnant. She went there to give birth to Yvonne. In September, Maurice started his school year in Welkenraedt, where he lived with family friends Patricia and Martin. He spent the weekends with our maternal aunt Agnès, who was then a student in Verviers. He returned to her home the following school year when he began high school (grades 7 to 12).

As for me, as long as I can remember, the first thing that comes to mind and that struck me is the morning call to prayer at the mosque. I can also remember the neighbor's tree—a neighbor who generously provided us with grapes—and the taste of dates and oranges (I could consume a few pounds, it seems). I also have memories of the little friends in the neighborhood, as well as the song of *Jamahiriya*, the name given to the government of Libya by Muammar Gaddafi. The song was often chanted in the streets.

In July 1983, I was six and when summer holidays began, Mom left for Belgium for a few months to give birth to Josiane.

Dad tried to organize a certain routine at home, but some evenings were chaotic. After long afternoons of playing with the neighbors, we first had to go to the shower, which I took at the same time as Denise. Dad was more flexible than Mom because we could stay in the water for a long time, but I didn't like it when he put an exfoliating glove on my back. I felt like he was tearing my skin off. I had the impression of being brand new each time I got out of the bath.

While we put on our pajamas, Dad went to the kitchen to prepare the meal (in the evenings when we didn't eat spaghetti with tomato sauce or large Moroccan flatbread with soup and eggs). He didn't fuss around. He always took a big saucepan and poured in all the ingredients one by one; meat with potatoes, then he added vegetables towards the end. It's called *igisafuriya* in Kinyarwanda, which means pan-mix everything. It "went down!"

Yvonne, who was just two years old, was a total "drama queen" who cried all the time for nothing. She gave Dad a hard time. I can still picture our poor dad trying unsuccessfully to soothe her while he was cooking, carrying her on his back with Mom's *ingobyi* cloth. I remember one evening when we all sat down at the table she burst into tears. Our exhausted father opened the door to put her out on the porch for a few seconds. From that day on, she no longer dared cry at the table for fear of finding herself alone behind the door.

I will never forget the first time I met the Libyan head of state. Dad had to go see Colonel Muammar Gaddafi, and he couldn't leave me alone at home. I think my sister Denise had gone to an activity, accompanied by Yvonne and Spéciose, my father's niece who lived with us. He dressed me in a blue dress with a white collar and asked me to put on little white lace socks before putting on my ballet flats. Then he prepared me for our interview with our distinguished host. He told me that this gentleman was very important and that I had to be good. I shouldn't ask for anything but wait for it to be offered to us. We then had a burgundy Mercedes, and for the first time I was allowed to ride in front in the passenger seat next to Dad, who was driving. The drive must have been short. I remember that the only thing I saw was the Mercedes symbol on the hood. I tried not to forget Dad's recommendations.

When we arrived, soldiers carried out the identity and vehicle check before opening the wide gates. We drove a few meters between palm trees, and finally we saw a huge building in front of us. A person invited us to get out of the car and took the vehicle key while a butler led us into a majestic living room, asking us in French to please wait. I had never seen such beautiful rooms except in the movies, and I, who found our velvet living room chairs large and soft, discovered that it was possible to have even bigger and more silky ones. Finally, the same butler led us to another room, even more beautiful, where there was a man with curly hair. Dad greeted him with a bow of his head, a gesture that this gentleman returned to him. I understood that we were in front of the famous Colonel Gaddafi. There was a tray of the most appetizing cakes of all kinds, and a beautiful golden carafe which must have contained tea. I waited wisely for our host to invite me to touch the tray of sweets.

Meanwhile, a lady dressed in an immaculate white apron served us tea, raising and lowering the teapot in a fluid gesture. I remained frozen like a statue throughout their meeting. I only remember that the pastries were exquisite and that I was rather full when I left.

A few months later, I accompanied Dad on a road trip from Tripoli to Djerba in Tunisia. I don't remember why he had to go there, but I know it was a long trip, and he told me to sing loudly so as not to fall asleep. So we sang together. It remains one of my best memories with him. He loved to challenge us. And his military side pushed him to reward us. That day I got a huge cotton candy when we were halfway there. We came back at night, and he told me to sleep …

Denise describes the Libyan period as marked by a golden childhood. She was in the same class in the French elementary school as her best friend, Zaïnab, who was from Mali. They spent their free time together. Dad had apparently rekindled our family tradition from Belgium of going to restaurants on the weekends. So every Sunday at noon, we went to lunch in a large restaurant that served a huge buffet with varied dishes. I remember there was a huge chocolate fountain in which we had fun dipping our fingers. Denise also remembers our car trips to Tunisia, the music on a loop in the background. She and I had fun counting cars or making funny faces at passers-by.

In fact, we didn't do many crazy things. Getting our ears pulled was the most common punishment and it was enough to dissuade us.

Denise also remembers the happy moments during the long holidays in Rwanda. She too had discovered the exotic charm of staying with our grandparents, and the shock of coming across big cockroaches or huge rats. There is still that first time she had to pee in rustic Turkish toilets without a bowl, *umusarani* in Kinyarwanda, which had to be used while squatting.

2. Return to Rwanda

The Discovery Years

From 1984 to 1987

Dad was recalled to Rwanda in 1984. The whole family left Libya at the end of June, Dad, Mom, Denise (ten years old), me, Alice (seven years old), Yvonne (three years old), and Josiane (one year old).

We settled into a beautiful house tucked away in downtown Kiyovu, in the heart of Kigali. It had a small fountain and a sloping garden. I can't forget that detail since I fell off my bike there several times.

The Rwandan climate was very special. It was mild and tropical but sometimes it rained heavily. It was very cold in some areas, such as the North. The red earth gave off an odor that only local people could recognize. The hills that were visible throughout the country marked the landscape wherever we looked.

Maurice came home in the summer of 1984 so he could go to the Saint-André high school in Kigali. He was to start his second year of high school. Even though we saw him regularly during the summer holidays, we were delighted to have all the siblings reunited again. Unfortunately, very quickly, his tropical allergy problems resurfaced! This second attempt to settle in a warm country with the whole family was unsuccessful. Not wanting to repeat a bad experience and knowing everything Maurice had gone through, my parents had to resign themselves to sending him back to Belgium to continue school.

Having lived mainly abroad since birth, we understood our mother tongue Kinyarwanda, but did not speak it. It was hard to live with at the beginning because we couldn't always make ourselves understood. The truth being reputed to come out of the mouths of children, those we met were not always nice to us. They made fun of our *bazungu* ("white") accent when we tried to speak Kinyarwanda.

So that we could get used to the language, our parents enrolled Denise and me in the primary school of Rugunga and Yvonne in kindergarten, where teaching was entirely in Kinyarwanda. At the same time, our parents hired a tutor who came to teach us to speak the national language. Kinyarwanda is a very complex language, where the consonants follow each other, and pronunciation is sometimes unpredictable.

For Denise, going to primary school in Rugunga was a shock, mainly due to the language barrier. However, she quickly integrated into a group of friends, which made her schooling easier, especially since she only stayed there for grades five and six. She remembers wearing the blue uniform and also getting her hands slapped with sticks, which was the Rwandan form of discipline. Some teachers, including the most remembered Mrs. Chantal and Mr. Muzehe, marked us. Mr. Muzehe, whose name means "the old man," perhaps because he had prematurely gray hair, impressed us with his size and charisma.

But all in all, it was a carefree time.

My first experience at the school in Rugunga was traumatic, especially when I learned that I had to wear a uniform, cut my hair, and remove my earrings. That ran against my natural style. After resisting for a few days , I had to give in and follow the rules like everyone else.

The first day when we were supposed to play some sports, I arrived at school proudly dressed in a dance tutu that Mom had had the "good" idea of getting me to wear. I had to put up with the teasing of my comrades. This did not facilitate integration because I was already considered a little *muzungu* or a "white" person. All the others were in shorts and t-shirts, and I couldn't imagine what my mother was thinking.

Nonetheless, I quickly made girlfriends. My first friend was the late Liliane Seburikoko. Her parents ran a super-market, and Liliane often brought sweets to share. Her mother was very beautiful, kind, and sweet. Our parents very soon allowed us to socialize outside of school. I remember those Wednesday afternoons when I was allowed to go home with Liliane and her mother. We first went to their place for lunch and then spent a few hours in their shop tasting all the novelties imported from Europe. I take this opportunity to pay tribute to the Seburikoko family, who was massacred at the Ndera orphanage a few years later in 1994. When I dared to watch the news about Rwanda on TV, I saw footage showing many people, including Liliane's mom and dad, begging to be picked up because they feared for their lives. The same reporter showed the images of corpses soon after. We thought for a long time that Liliane had survived somehow, since she wasn't in that footage. Such were the hopeful rumors. Rugunga alumni with whom I am in contact confirmed to me later that unfortunately she was dead. Rest in peace, Liliane. I will never forget you, just as I will never forget your beautiful and sweet mother.

Little by little, I widened my circle of friends, which made my integration easier: Chantal, Angélique, Gisèle, Rosine, Ingrid, Madudu, Capitoline, and Louise, whom we nicknamed *Souris* (mouse), she was so frail ...

Slowly but surely, I began to master Kinyarwanda, a language that we started to practice at home as well.

One day, while I was likely in third grade, our teacher asked us what our ethnic group was. What was she talking about? I knew absolutely nothing about it! First of all, what did "ethnicity" mean? Then, she asked the children to raise their hands when they heard their ethnicity. I remember then that I raised my hand each time when she mentioned the Hutus, the Tutsis, and the Twas. So, she said to me, exasperated, "What's your last name?" I replied, "Nsabimana." She replied that that was fine, and she knew in which ethnic group to classify me. We talked about it during recess, and my friends said they heard that some were meaner than others ... It was intriguing for me as an eight-year-old ...

Back home, I told my parents what had happened, and then I asked them what I was. They told me that we were *Hutus*. You can surely imagine what the next question was. What difference was there between my *Tutsi* or *Twa* classmates and me? I remember however that there were none in the *Twa* "category" in our class.

Mom asked me if I had noticed any differences between us. My answer was no.

I also asked if it was true that there were more villains in one group than in another. I will never forget Dad's response, who explained that there was no difference between us because, as Rwandans, we had a common language and culture. So being reassured, I did not try to find out more. He added that he would tell us the history of our families in detail later.

During the 1985 Easter holidays, Mom left for Belgium for a few months to give birth to Fabrice. This time it was easier for Dad logistically. There were house staff to take care of the house and the kitchen. In addition, Denise and I took our roles as big sisters to Yvonne and Josiane seriously.

At school, as in life, I was a very calm and patient person. But that didn't mean that I would put up with everything. One day, a classmates called Norbert tested my limits. He must have laughed at the scars on my legs. When we returned to Rwanda, I developed pimples on my body, leaving me with ugly scars that embarrassed me when I was little. Mom had the magic concoction to remedy that, it was Palmer's, a cosmetic cocoa butter balm. As much as the antibiotic Bactrim was the solution to every ailment, so was Palmer's balm part of our childhood. My mother always buys it everywhere, and her grandchildren have already had it smeared on their bodies. Personally, I put so much on that I can still smell it, even without applying it.

In short, I first made fun of Norbert's stupid remarks, letting him talk and asking him nicely to stop. But already, my friends and I found boys our age immature. To start with, we were taller. But he was particularly "short-legged." So, after yet another warning, I grabbed him by the hands and twirled him around the playground. Then on another occasion, I threw him on the ground. I was of course punished. I had to remain on my knees in the schoolyard for the entire recess while my friends were having fun.

My education at the Rugunga school continued peacefully after that incident, and I became an expert in Kinyarwanda. We had built a small world inside the school that we called *Kamembe* where we played during recess. It was a green space in an alley of the playground. We used trees and foliage to make little houses. We had everything needed for a nice break. We sat on the leaves and chatted or even shared our snacks. It was the perfect time to tell each other little secrets. Our friendships were changing. Small groups developed and then fell apart, but always in a good-natured spirit.

That is how the school year ended. Mom came home with Fabrice shortly after the start of the summer holidays.

We often visited our parents' hometowns during holidays or long weekends. Dad and Mom felt it was important that we connect with their roots to understand that we should never forget where we came from, despite the fact we were born with better conditions than they had. They often told us that although we had everything we needed, we should never take anything for granted. Above all, we should be able to adapt to all conditions and be grateful for what we have, not knowing what tomorrow might bring. And they were right ...

We had our little routine. We started with visits to my paternal grandmother's home in Ruhengeri. These visits, which were anything but glamorous, remain among the happiest memories of our childhood. Life there was simple, made up of good times spent together.

It all started with the car. Sometimes we traveled in the burgundy Mercedes 230 E. Other times we took our white Toyota pick-up truck. Our parents said it was the most practical because the tires would resist the winding roads better and we could also transport clothing to distribute to village children or bring food for our grandparents. As children we much preferred traveling by car. When we were in the pick-up, we were ashamed because we felt like we were traveling like goats. The domestics put a mattress down to cushion the shock and a blanket. Next to it they put a few bags of green bananas from our farm and various exotic fruit that we brought over for the family. We always crossed our fingers not to meet anyone we knew while traveling through the capital Kigali.

We were at the end of the summer of 1985. The road seemed horribly long, especially for Yvonne and Josiane. Fabrice, who was still only a baby, slept almost the entire first trip. To keep Yvonne and Josiane busy, Denise and I asked them to name the brands and colors of cars and count them. We would also get them to say "Hi," or to make faces to passengers in other cars. Mobile screens were not yet in fashion. We also had fun telling them scary stories, making them believe that ghosts or evil spirits were hiding in the trees or prowling the road.

Halfway there, we systematically stopped at Nyirangarama, located halfway to the Ruhengeri road. We would buy food from peasant merchants who sold *sambusas* or the famous hot donuts that were the pride of the region. There was also the Ruhengeri market, where we inevitably bought goat meat to take back to Grandma's.

We then began the second part of the trip. About ten kilometers before arriving at Ryinyo, the hill where Dad came from, the roads became very difficult. It was the part that wasn't paved. As we got closer to our destination, the roads became even more winding, narrow, and muddy and there was no guard rail. Suffice it to say that the slightest mistake could have cost us our lives. But Dad navigated through with confidence. We were still scared, and it was always a great relief when we finally arrived.

We all had our preferences. The little ones preferred the stay with our paternal grandmother in Ruhengeri; they were always excited at the idea of going there. Dad adored his mother, and she loved him. It should be remembered that he was her only son.

His mother, Marcianne Nyirambona, born in 1910, lived in a small house perched at the top of a hill. A gate led to a small courtyard where Grandmother liked to sit and where there were two small houses. It looked like one of them was only used when her children and grandchildren came to visit. I never quite understood where she slept. She always slipped away discreetly around eight in the evening, and we would see her again the next day when we woke up.

From her home, the view of the valley was breathtaking, peaceful, and majestic. The air was very pure there. She was always wearing a military beret and her traditional dress consisting of a long-checkered skirt, a blue sweater, a large necklace of red beads, and multiple copper wire bracelets twisted around *Ibitare* or cow's hair, meant to protect against arthritis. She also had her tobacco pipe. We always wondered if she wore the same clothes or had several sets. She loved to walk barefoot, and every time we visited her, we tried to imitate her. However, we gave up very quickly after stepping on gravel or tripping over some exotic trees with thorny leaves. Grandmother had both a serious and mischievous look. She was still walking with her cane, her back bent as if carrying all the misfortune in the world. From time to time, Dad would ask her to straighten up. She would then sit up straight, saying proudly: "You see that I know how to do it." She lived in simple conditions. Her village had neither electricity nor drinking water within easy reach.

As soon as Dad entered his childhood home, he would change completely and relax. He loved to sit with his peers and roll up his sleeves to show us where to fetch water for Grandma, breathe in the fresh, clean air deeply with *impungure*. In short, he swapped his official uniform for a simple shirt and met the local people.

The roosters crowing would wake us up very early. Just like Maurice when he was very little, Yvonne and I liked to go and get water with the person who worked at our grandmother's house. We brought it back but usually spilled half of it on the way. When we got back, the court-yard would already be full of people who had learned that the child prodigy had returned to the village. Dad, who had managed to wash up with water that we found freezing, was already outside, chatting with everyone. He invited us to come and sit down to listen and get to know everyone. Dad was in his element, simple, talking with each of them and discreetly handing them small amounts of money as they came by.

We often left them chatting and joined the maid who would have heated up some water for us so we could take a shower behind the house. There was no modern toilet but somewhere behind the house there was a large rectangular-shaped dug-out hole inspired by a Turkish toilet. The first time we had to pee, it was difficult to connect the urge to urinate and this improbable hole. I held back the first time but couldn't take it anymore, so I went back. Fearful of being surprised in this uncomfortable situation, I peed all over myself. It seems that Denise was even stronger when she was little. During a visit to Rwanda, she peed in an *ikibindi calabash* used to make sorghum beer. What a crime!

In the afternoons, we could play outside with kids from the village. It was the first initiation to the traditional Rwandan dance, particularly the *Ikinimba*: a typical vigorous dance in Northern Rwanda, and the famous *Hinga amasaka* which means cultivate sorghum, sung and danced on every important family event. Then we would explore the surroundings. Dad wanted us to follow in his footsteps to visit his older sister, Généreuse, and his uncles, who lived not far away. We were well received everywhere, always with the traditional sorghum-based drink, *umusururu*, and something to eat. Those who cooked more modernly prepared a platter of fried potatoes with goat meat.

Sometimes we just stayed at home. I have a clear image of Dad helping his mother peel the potatoes and every last bit of peel had to be removed. Grandma hated delegating this task because she didn't want anything to be wasted.

Then the basket of peelings was taken out of the house and thrown into the field where the goats and sheep fed on them.

The whole family gathered in the evening in a small room at the back of the yard. We sat down to eat a mixture of beans and dried corn, the traditional *impungure* dish that dad seemed to love. But the more we ate it the more we came to appreciate it. We would occasionally be entitled to a goat that Grandmother sacrificed in our honor from among her herd or one that we brought back from the Ruhengeri market. The *umufa* goat broth was specially reserved for Dad. And once the animal had been eaten, Grandmother would show us the goat she was saving for her only son's next visit. During the meal, Dad liked to tell us stories of his youth. Grandmother also told him all about her daily life; who had come to visit her, what problems different people had. After eating, the adults usually remained around the fire. The younger ones however would slip away inside the house, along with Grandmother, after she smoked her last pipe.

Our parents occupied a room in the second house, which was opened especially for visits, while the children slept in another room. As we were afraid, we liked to sleep close together. Above the bed hung bundles of sorghum that Grandma was drying to make *ikigage* or sorghum beer.

Nights were terribly cold—temperatures in the North hovered around fifteen degrees Celsius—plus you could hear the rats running around. Having observed them during the day, I was convinced they could be harmful. They didn't hesitate to charge at us and stare at us, at least that was my impression.

For the second part of the stay, we went to Gisenyi, where Mom comes from. Sometimes Dad would encourage us to walk from Nkuli (Ruhengeri) to Karago (Gisenyi), two towns about fourteen kilometers apart. We were to leave at dawn, accompanied by a few cousins or by Dad himself. Before leaving, we were given a cane to help us during the climbs. We took small paths where we could observe small natural rivers.

As we went down towards Gisenyi, it was possible to see the Mount Nyiragongo volcano (3,470 meters or 11,300 feet) from afar. The hills were tough to climb. Finally, more than two hours later, we reached these rocks, which gave us a clue that we were almost at our destination. We often reached Rurembo, the hill where Mom was born, before those who had gone by car. This just shows the bad state of the roads.

The first stays in Rurembo were less exotic. The place was in a sense "more civilized." Our maternal grandparents' house was very modern for its time. We even ate eggs and good free-range chicken!

Grandfather, Ntumahe Vénérand, was not tall. We have always seen him dressed up. Grandmother Mélanie was slim, with mischievous eyes, and was always dressed in the traditional Rwandan *umukenyero* outfit and with a colorful headscarf. They both looked younger than our paternal grandmother. We loved playing in their yard. We would visit Mom's extended family. At the time, she still had her grandmother, our great-grandmother, whom we would visit, and our paternal aunt, Dative.

Everything was authentic in the mountains of the North: the people, the clean air, the local food, the magnificent landscapes with the hills, the cliffs, and the smell of red earth after the rain ... We learned to appreciate everything at its true value when we were a little older.

1988

Early in the year, Dad was appointed head of the military camp and training center for non-commissioned officers in Bugesera, located in eastern Rwanda, about fifty kilometers from Kigali, on the northern border of Burundi. During his assignment, which lasted two years, we would often travel back-and-forth between the capital and Bugesera. We went there on a few weekends and during the holidays. Life was quite pleasant, and we had a fairly lively social life there. In short, it was a somewhat bizarre period, halfway between a normal life and a feeling of exoticism.

When we arrived, fresh tilapia and grilled goat meat were waiting for us. Denise and I liked collecting freshly baked bread right out of the oven near Camp Gako's kitchen. Many other kids of people in the military came from Kigali to spend weekends with their fathers like us. Yvonne quickly made friends with children of her generation and had soon explored the entire military camp. She often asked for a few coins to buy candy in the only shop that sold sweets. Then, accompanied by her friends, Yvonne would walk around the camp. She got her bearings very quickly. The children moved about together, going from house to house, and the parents often would be in touch with each other to keep track of them!

We had a very large house, but the layout was not great. A long corridor, like in hotels, led to all the rooms. And the bathrooms were completely isolated from the rest. We were surrounded by trees and a long forest. Nobody dared venture outside at night because, in addition to frogs, there were often large snakes, though they were not poisonous. One day we saw one in the house. I don't remember who told us we had to cross our legs and arms under our chests and not move to prevent the snake from biting us! Looking back on it, I tell myself, what nonsense!

The little ones liked to play outside. Our wise baby sister Josiane walked her dolls while Fabrice played soccer. Yvonne loved climbing trees. One day, Josiane brought back a piece of the Thermos that Mom loved so much and that had disappeared. Mom had first suspected the house helpers but finally understood that Yvonne, after confessing, had broken it and then buried it behind the garden for fear of getting punished. Yvonne was our Miss Mischief. Even though she was breaking a lot of things, she had stopped whining as she grew, bringing a lot of cheerfulness into the house.

One day, however, Yvonne got overzealous. It was a December weekend. We had a family tradition of preparing the Christmas tree together the weekend before Christmas. Yvonne, who had been told to come back in the early afternoon, arrived just as Dad was hanging the last star on top of the tree. She was shaking from head to toe, aware that she had overstepped her bounds. We can still see Dad, in shorts, coming down the ladder and Yvonne trying to run away. In two steps, he caught her by the arm, laughing. He was proud of his little explorer and gave her everything. In fact, Dad often threatened to punish us but never did.

We knew how far we could push it. Only when the vein bulged in Dad's temple or his gaze suddenly hardened did we know we had to calm down.

Even far away, Dad was very picky and demanding that we do well in school. Whenever we had to show our report cards, it was always stressful. We would wait to see him on the weekend to get him to sign it. He scrutinized it line by line. Over time it got better. A tutor came to the house to help us with a few subjects because Mom couldn't do everything independently while Dad was away.

A few months after Dad moved to Bugesera, there was an outbreak of measles in the military camp. Josiane and

I caught it. I remember being very weak and barely able to walk. In the evening, I hallucinated. I told Denise I would die. We gradually recovered. When it came to health issues, I was the least lucky; a few months before, I had had malaria. I had also had trouble with amoeba before and caught the mumps too.

My first experience in a bar was in Bugesera. At that time, we were living with our cousin Louise, who was in her twenties. Since I always liked hanging out with older people, I remember that one evening I went out with two young ladies, Louise and her friend Valérie, who happened to be going out with Samuel, a cousin of Dad's. Samuel had taken us to eat goat and tripe brochettes, known as *zingaro*, served with grilled bananas in tomato sauce. I hadn't asked permission, since I didn't think I was risking anything going out with Samuel and the older girls. In fact, I had spent a lovely evening listening with interest to the discussions while sipping my Sprite. When we got home, Dad was waiting for us. He called me into the living room and struck up a conversation I will never forget.

Dad: How old are you?

Me: Twelve.

Dad: How many years are there in high school?

Me: Six (I must have been in Secondary One).

Dad: So, you think that just after you start high school, you can go and shake it up with the grown-ups instead of concentrating on your homework?

Obviously, I had no answer nor anyone to defend me. So, it was between Dad and me.

He had this natural authority. From that day on, I understood where my limits were and how far my dreams and fantasies could take me. I then knew how to limit my requests to go to parties, birthdays, and pajama parties ...

If my future hosts failed to provide the necessary information, I had to prepare a detailed agenda, the equivalent of an invitation with all the details of the event: address, start and end time, and parents' phone number. This taught me to be "disciplined" when I was sent out into the world. Thank you, Dad!

During the Christmas holidays, we left our residence in Kiyovu to move to Ndera, a small town on the outskirts of the urban area of Kigali, about fifteen kilometers from the capital. Our parents had built a huge property nestled in greenery and surrounded by fields. The organization of the move was not easy to plan with Dad living in Bugesera. But I do remember that he had taken a few days off to come and take care of everything with Mom.

1989

We were all excited about moving. The green space of the land was carefully divided in two. On one side were vegetables and fruit of all kinds. On the other, there was a flower garden and behind the fence banana trees and a small farm with cows, hens, and rabbits.

Traveling back and forth from our home in Ndera to the school in downtown Kigali was taking more and more time, so we spent the first few months getting used to the new morning rush without really having time to enjoy the house.

During the Easter holidays in April, we were finally able to really discover our new environment. Being always outside and playing barefoot in nature is something you can't forget. Fabrice, Josiane, and Yvonne spent hours outdoors, picking half-ripe strawberries and apples, which were very sour because they weren't planted in their natural environment. There was no comparison with the ones we occasionally tasted when Mom brought them back from the Ali Rwanda supermarket. The three young ones played until Cyrille, our cleaning man and cook, came to call them to eat. The main reason we haven't forgotten about him is because he had such huge feet. Apparently, he wore at least size 17 shoes which meant he needed custom-made shoes. That's why he walked barefoot most of the time.

We had a Doberman-type dog called Minouche, a name borrowed from our former Libyan cat that Mom wanted to reuse as a souvenir, even though a sweet little name like that really didn't match the size of the dog. Fabrice, Josiane, and Yvonne always had fun going over to his cage and feeding him leftovers, then running away laughing to hide they were scared of his barking. When our father came home, he would open the cage and pet the dog in front of us, giving it a drink of fresh milk from the day. But that didn't make us less afraid of touching or patting him. He was anything but domesticated and seemed to obey only his true master, Dad.

Matata, our other household helper, went to milk the cows very early in the morning, *gukama amata*. We can still see him sitting on a small stool with a bucket under the cow's udder, singing religious songs repeatedly. He began by grasping a teat in each hand, which he maneuvered with a simple squeeze, carefully angling the bucket to collect the milk. When we got up, we would often drink this fresh milk, obtained by *ikivuguto* fermentation. We also ate the eggs our hens had laid. For dessert, we had the choice of exotic fruit such as guavas, bananas, pineapples or papayas, straight out of our large tropical garden. Everything was obviously "organic."

Relations between our three musketeers, Yvonne, Josiane, and Fabrice, at home, varied. Though sometimes friendly, they would become respectful when it was the "cold war." They spent a lot of time playing marbles in yard. Fabrice loved playing Ninjas with Josiane or his best friend Ghislain, alias Dumu. They made masks from Dad's old military sweaters or his old t-shirts.

They also loved watching cartoons like *Tom & Jerry* or *Mickey Mouse*. In the evening, when they didn't fall asleep from fatigue, they would join Dad in the living room to watch films featuring Louis de Funès or Jean-Paul Belmondo, two of his favorite actors. They didn't have to understand what was being said. Everyone laughed until tears ran down their faces. I can't remember how many times we watched the entire *Gendarmes* collection, the great classics like *La Grande Vadrouille, Rabbi Jacob,* or even *The Professional, The Bridge on the River Kwai, Spartacus, Les Uns et les Autres* [Boléro] .... ! We watched these movies so many times that we damaged the VHS tapes. I even once surprised Yvonne trying to put the films back together from the videos that had finally given up the ghost through wear and tear.

The house was never calm with the three musketeers. One day, when Yvonne apparently really got on Fabrice's nerves, Fabrice replied by throwing a brick at her head. I don't know if the brick reached the target, but I watched it all from my bedroom as Fabrice chased Yvonne to try to catch her. Of course, I was used to seeing this kind of scene, so I didn't even pay attention to it.

On one rainy day, all five of us were outside with our cousin Béatrice. We were watching the rabbits and chickens in front of our little farm. Fabrice, who always loved nature and was still so young and innocent, had let himself be carried away by his thoughts while looking at the flock of hens. He kept repeating: *inkoko, inkoko* . . . (chicken).

Suddenly, turning around, there was nobody to be seen. We had all left him to his dreams. He completely panicked and cried as he ran away. We had hidden behind the trees just to scare him. It may seem cruel, but we knew very well that there was no risk since our home had a fence around it. In any case he was the first to know all the possible and unimaginable hiding places.

On weekends, we often visited our aunt Julienne, Dad's older sister, who lived in Masaka, not far from Ndera. Her house was surrounded by fields of banana trees. Her children were not the same age as us. We got along with our cousins. Béatrice, the eldest, lived with us during the week. Yosefa, the youngest, was of the same generation as Fabrice. They played together all the time, running through the fields and playing hide-and-seek, sometimes stopping to get some drinking water somewhere behind their property. Before nightfall, they reappeared miraculously. Before we hit the road, Aunt Julienne always prepared and packed delicious corn grilled over a wood fire for us.

Maurice, who was studying in Germany, always came to visit us during the summer holidays. That year he was planning to stay longer than usual, four months. He had just finished high school and was waiting to find out which country might grant him a scholarship for higher education. It ended up being the polytechnic university of Graz in Austria that accepted him. But he was not to start until the following academic year.

As usual, when he was planning to come back during the summer, we all took great care to write him letters with drawings a few months before his arrival so that he knew exactly what to bring us. Fabrice had scribbled drawings of cars. Josiane, our Miss Sentimental and Fashionista, drew dolls she surrounded with pretty hearts for "Molice" (in

Kinyarwanda, the L and R sounds are the same). Yvonne, our tomboy, would ask for motorcycles. I told all the news I heard on the radio and family news, and I concluded, of course, by asking for a camera and stylish t-shirts. As for Denise, she talked about her problems as a teenager without forgetting to end her letters by asking for earrings, caps, and, of course, chocolate.

In mid-June, poor Maurice had arrived laden with gifts (trying his best to fulfill our wishes). He would have chocolates, toys, and video cassettes with the latest hits from American singers. We had a great summer together, dancing to MC Hammer and Salt-N-Pepa! He always brought Denise and me accessories we thought were cool, like bandanas, caps, and sunglasses.

Since we were all living in the sun year-round, we would always ask him what the snow looked like and how it felt to touch it. Besides, for Denise and I who were older, the last years spent abroad were in Tripoli, where it was just as hot. We had forgotten the effect of the cold because we were too small to remember when we lived in Belgium. And having only tasted tropical fruit, we wondered what typical Nordic fruit tasted like.

At the Gako military camp in Bugesera, Fabrice, and his friend Serge spent the first years of their childhood totally carefree, playing with helicopters made from tree branches. Since we were lucky enough to have nannies which allowed Mom the luxury of being quite present thanks to her job as a merchant, Fabrice had not needed to go to the daycare.

He had also just spent the summer running and exploring every corner of our new property on his bike, taking advantage of the presence of his older brother (whom he took for an uncle) to teach him some techniques and other games. Today he remembers a few stories that marked him during this period that was calm for everyone and that contributed to forging an image of his father as a rock or savior. One day, when he went with Dad to visit a family, he remembers that it was raining outside, and that he was playing football with the two children. He was hit in the face with a soccer ball. Fabrice recalls the water-soaked ball giving him more intense pain from the friction and the speed at which it hit his face. He screamed and vividly remembers Dad running to comfort him and see what had happened. He remembers the cold cloth he applied to his nose, asking him to keep calm.

I remember having organized many parties at home that summer. My parents had friends from all walks of life: *Hutus, Tutsis,* and *Twas* (the third ethnic group which is not discussed much), southerners, northerners, rich, poor, and white! Today, it is a legacy we carry within us, and we are very grateful to our parents for that. So many people dropped by the house just to say hello or came on Sundays after mass. Dad left us this unconditional love that we share with our siblings.

What's more, when we talk with people from all backgrounds, we have always had a positive reaction. Many tell us that Dad helped them somehow or housed them while they were students, etc. He indeed loved people; he always tried to give whatever he could, either by opening doors or giving a little of his time. He had loyal friends, such as his best friend, Gasongero. When he came to our house with his family or when we went to their house, we knew it would be a gastronomic weekend filled with tears and laughter. Seeing the two fathers greet each other was already quite a spectacle. As soon as they saw each other, they laughed like two kids and traded endless jokes. Gasongero had kids our age, so we also had time to keep busy while the two good friends were in a world of their own. We sometimes went to sleep, leaving them there talking, only to find them in the same place in the morning. I'm sure they met in the heavens (may they rest in peace) to continue their friendship and joke again.

Dad resumed his back-and-forth trips between Bugesera and Ndera. We visited him whenever we could, and also visited our grandparents.

When he came home for a few days, he resumed his ritual of jogging before lunch and then taking a quick shower. He would come to the table with his towel wrapped around his hips and after a light lunch took a micro nap. He then reviewed all the issues that he had not been able to complete the previous days.

During his short stays, we prepared his favorite dishes for him. He loved, among other things, red beans and boiled potatoes. I was always happy to cook his "medium rare" steak as he liked it. He would then give me a mark ranging from one to ten; it was usually a nine! If at home he liked his steak "medium-rare," he preferred it "medium" in the French restaurant where we went from time to time on Sundays after mass. He always started by cutting small pieces so that whoever wanted to taste it could do so, then he could enjoy it quietly without anyone hovering around him. As an accompaniment, there was always his very fresh "tonic." As for Mom, she took the time to cook us baked bananas or lasagna, two of our favorite weekend dishes. As I loved to cook, I always got close to her to observe how she did it. Besides, I wanted to study hospitality and become a chef. I had even spoken to the owner of the French restaurant because I wanted to take practical cooking lessons. There was also Alexandre, who worked as a service provider at the Hotel des Mille Collines and who had told me about the profession of maître d'hôtel. But Dad had put an end to that dream. One evening, after having a few drinks at the military camp with his colleagues, he came home with red eyes and was a bit tipsy. He then called me and asked me to sit down to explain to him if I thought he foresaw his children, for whom he paid a fortune in school, becoming "cooks!"

Like everyone else, Dad obviously had his flaws. The most striking was that he enjoyed drinking from time to time with his close friends or colleagues. When he drank too much, Dad had a keen ear and a sharp eye. He had this annoying art of observing us, letting us do what we wanted including stupidities that we thought were well hidden, that is until he brought everything out to us when he had been drinking. The times he drank were stressful for us, especially because, oddly enough, he seemed to become more lucid, or more at ease saying things he wouldn't normally say and that we believed to be secret. His perfectionist side was exacerbated in these moments. He then put us in front of a fait accompli, like during that unforgettable evening when he ended my dream of studying in the hotel industry. Since we knew he knew, there was no escape other than confession.

However, he never got drunk enough to lose control of himself. Sometimes he came to our rooms to wake us up and meet us in the living room. His red eyes stared at us. Then, with a steady gaze, he went from one to the other, reminding us of the lies we thought we had hidden or of our subterfuges, or even scolding us about our behavior towards each other or Mom. He took the opportunity to give us moral lessons.

It happened in particular to Denise, who, during that school year, had invented a new Wednesday afternoon activity: computer classes that she was supposed to attend with her friends, Maryse and Edinath. Instead of this activity, the small group went to shake it up at *"Boums"* (afternoon dance parties) at Eden Garden, a trendy little cafe in downtown Kigali. Naively, she thought she was fooling Dad until, one day, he had a few drinks and told her he knew about her little Wednesday games, even though he wasn't there.

Fortunately, he completely quit drinking during his last years of life.

Social life was also punctuated by both drama and joy. That summer, Anisia, Mom's little sister, lost her husband, Aminadab. Together with Dad, the two sisters naturally agreed that within our large, united family, Mom would take her niece Claudine in, which would give her mother the time to organize the mourning and look after the other five children.

It was like having a little doll at home for us. When she landed in the family, she was very shy and hardly spoke, but she knew how to be heard when necessary. Josiane, the youngest of the girls, immediately took Claudine under her wing. This meant she no longer had to impose upon Fabrice and Dumu but had someone she could quietly play dolls with. It was perfect, especially since Yvonne was then spending time with her cousins and girlfriends of the same age. They already thought of themselves as teenagers and liked chatting in our little bungalow in the middle of the garden.

In September, when Fabrice started kindergarten in the same school as us in Rugunga, he hated it from day one. The school routine was like the end of a long recess for him. He now had to wake up early because it took at least thirty minutes to get from Ndera to Rugunga. He remembers

spending most of his time playing on the swing and running around, especially during recess. He and his friends
King, Pappy, and Belinda were like the four fingers of a
hand, and they spent most of their time together. All three
boys loved Belinda and did everything to get her to notice
them. Sometimes they bickered over who she liked best.

Fabrice had a hard time adjusting to this new way of life.
It got worse when he turned five. It was always a struggle for
my poor Mom or anyone in my family to convince him to
go to school. My aunt Julienne sometimes managed when
she was staying with us. With her, he didn't dare say no.
Once at school, he often threw tantrums and cried, begging
me to take him home. He would sob in front of the school
fence until he ran out of tears. In the end, he was practically
carried by force back into the schoolyard. In class, it was no
better. Sometimes the teacher would bring him back to my
class so that I could calm him down. When he got home
after a long day of school, our mother's breast was her only
remedy to calm him down. As a result, he was breastfed
until he was five years old!

As for Josiane and Yvonne, they were already in primary
school in Rugunga, which made it better for them.

Josiane, who was flirtatious and stylish even when she
was little, always wanted to wear the same dress. Uniforms
were compulsory in primary school. Girls had to wear
blue dresses, while boys wore a combination of a shirt and
khaki-colored shorts. Josiane adored her little indigo blue
dress with short sleeves and a Jackie Kennedy boat neck.
As she loved the chants and the bungee jumps that brought
up the red dust from the earth so much, her feet would be
almost orange when she came home.

In those days, we would take over our bungalow as a
play area. It was later transformed into a living space for

the many bodyguards who lived with us when the tension was at its height in the '90s.

It's the only thing that remained intact after the destruction of our home. We were moved to see that it had retained its soul twenty-five years later when our nephew Maxime brought us back a photo taken at the same place.

Maurice returned to Belgium in September to begin a preparatory year before entering university. When he would leave it always felt like a (sad) return to normal. We needed time to get back to our routine, which coincided with the start of the school year. His stories always made us want to visit Europe. Even though Denise and I had lived in Belgium, we had very few memories of it since we were still very young.

To motivate us to work hard, Dad often told us that as a reward the one who had the best marks at school would spend the summer holidays in Europe, *Mu buraya* in Kinyarwanda. Literally translated, it was almost like a one-way trip to a little earthly paradise. Fabrice thought that to get there, you had to go through Heaven, especially since the last time he flew was when he was a baby. So for him, going to Belgium meant climbing very high, like going to Heaven.

3. The upheaval (from 1990 to 1992)

1990

Maurice finished his preparatory year in June. He remembers that Dad told him not to come and spend the summer in Rwanda because tensions were high, and the political climate was uncertain. He, therefore, returned to our friends and his host family in Bonn Bad Godesberg, where he lived during July and August. They then left Germany at the same time. He went to Austria and the Niyonizeye family went to Rwanda, where they were returning to settle permanently after several years of service abroad.

For Fabrice, the situation improved in primary school right from the start in September. It was compulsory to wear a uniform (a beige shirt and trousers) and to have your hair cut short. Primary school teachers were very authoritarian; there was no question of showing any disrespect. Behavior had to be exemplary, or students would be punished. Mild punishment would include having to stand at the back of the class, while severe punishment might mean having your fingers slapped with a wooden or plastic stick or even having to kneel at the back of the class while holding a brick in each hand and remaining still for a few minutes. If you wanted to go to the bathroom or anything else you had to raise your hand and wait for permission.

The change was amazing. Fabrice had become an energetic child whose favorite subjects were mathematics—he loved and knew his multiplication tables by heart—and religion, including the catechism. However, tests induced panic and test results even more so. The teacher called everyone to the front of the class. Students who got marks above or equal to the average were isolated from those who did not pass and who often received collective punishment. The little ones had a way of reducing the pain. They would close their eyes and squeeze their buttocks. This all may seem barbaric and totally unthinkable in Western society, but it taught us to walk straight and be disciplined. All those who went through it laugh it off today and keep no aftermath or trauma.

Claudine returned to kindergarten in Rugunga, always well-behaved and under the close protection of her older sister Josiane. Yvonne lived her life. Everything was going well for the girls.

As for me, when I finished sixth grade at Rugunga elementary school, my parents thought it necessary for me to become reacquainted with French. I had grown reluctant to speak French since I had learned to master Kinyarwanda, probably out of fear of humiliation for not being understood by my friends. So, I was enrolled in the École belge de Kigali (Belgian School in Kigali) for high school where Denise had been studying for three years already.

Another shock was awaiting me when I arrived. French, my first mother tongue that I once spoke fluently, had disappeared or was completely buried. I had all the words in my mind, but a mental block prevented me from talking. As my Rwandan friends had made so much fun of my poor Kinyarwanda skills at Rugunga primary school, I had sworn to make up for my shortcomings to the detriment of French.

However, integration into the Belgian school was simpler and quicker. First, there was Denise, and her friends, who I thought were so cool. They met at the school cafeteria during breaks to discuss fashion and teen problems.

Then, I met a lot of my friends from primary school in Rugunga: Liliane, Chantal, Angélique, Gisèle, Moïse, Ingrid... Afterwards, a group formed very quickly with those already on-site or from another school: Patricia, Gustave, Corneille, Malaïka and more.

Fluency in French soon returned.

For lunch, we established a routine that allowed us to save time. Instead of returning to Ndera, about a half-hour from the city, our driver took us to Mom's shop in downtown Kigali. We ate lunch there and then went back to class. Mom had taken matters into her own hands during Dad's absence. She had developed *Univa*, her semi-wholesale and retail business.

On October 1, 1990, shortly after celebrating my thirteenth birthday, we heard on the radio during our lunch break that the Rwandan Patriotic Front (RPF) had invaded Rwanda from the north. The national radio announced that the armed wing of the RPF, made up of former Tutsi refugees, had invaded Rwanda. We used the terms *Inyenzi* and *Inkotanyi*.[1] At first, my school friends and I cluelessly thought they were a species of huge animals like in the movies. We did not understand why they were labeled "cockroaches!"

I remember we were scared and talked about it a lot. But in no time, the carefree young teenagers that we were quickly relegated "that" to the background, especially since it was happening miles away from us. We thought we were quite far away in Kigali, in the capital. As young people, we did not feel very concerned by the fighting that was taking place in the North as long as our daily life and our Kigali/Ndera/Bugesera routine had not (yet) been affected.

Maurice was not surprised when Dad called him early in October 1990 to tell him that the RPF had attacked Rwanda. Since the last great famine in Rwanda in the 1940s and internal political unrest in the late 1950s, many Rwandans emigrated to Congo and Uganda. The previous summer, a distant relative who had also emigrated to Uganda, where he had become a trader, had come to visit Dad when Maurice was with him at home in the Bugesera military camp. This gentleman told him he had heard of ongoing preparations. Rwandan refugees in Uganda were preparing to launch a military offensive against Rwanda ... Dad had taken this warning very seriously. After thorough investigations, he established the accuracy of the information and warned President Habyarimana.

---

1. *Inyenzi* is an acronym chosen by the group of rebels composed mainly of royalist exiles, who attacked Rwanda in the 1960s, to regain power following their flight after the 1959 Rwandan revolution.

A few weeks after the attack by the Rwandan Patriotic Army, Dad was called to go to the frontline in northern Rwanda where the fighting was raging. He wasn't even given time to pack his things. Maurice went to collect them nine months later, during his annual visit the following summer. During his helicopter ride from the Bugesera military camp, Dad had made a stopover for a *briefing* at the headquarters of the Rwandan Armed Forces in Kigali, where he was immediately put in command of the counter-offensive. He barely had time to tell Mom by phone. He was passing through but couldn't stop at home. The helicopter had flown that same day to the frontline.

We got used to no longer living with Dad regularly. He was transferred with no transition period to a place we were beginning to consider to be dangerous. As a result, we couldn't go visit him anymore and didn't know when we would be able to see him again.

The first time he could go on leave from the warzone to visit his family must have been shortly before the year-end holidays. It was a bittersweet visit. We tried to preserve the family tradition of decorating a Christmas tree, but the joy was not there. Dad didn't have the usual cheerfulness in his eyes. He tried his best to look natural, but we felt his mind was elsewhere. Nevertheless, we were so happy to see him and grateful to celebrate Christmas and New Year with family and some close friends that nothing else mattered. We even danced to classic hits with Boney M and Abba in the lead.

1991

It was a very difficult year for our immediate family. We didn't see Dad at all, and it was impossible for us to reach him on the phone or to go and meet him. This situation

THE LIFE OF THE NSABIMANA FAMILY   55

would get worse as war raged and promised to be long. At home, the fear was palpable.

We grew up in a Catholic family where all the stages of a Christian life were, and still are, important in the eyes of our parents. As children, we did not understand why we had to submit to these endless and sometimes boring catechism lessons. You had to be diligent and focused. With a military father, everything had to be done in an orderly and disciplined manner. Dad wasn't overly strict, but we had to be straightforward, including in our relationship with God. Mom and Dad taught us to pray and thank God every day. It was quite natural therefore that prayer became a refuge for him and us during this period.

During his long absences, faith comforted us. We feared for Dad because we knew he could be killed at any moment, but we also feared for our own lives. Gunshots were often heard in the city even though there was a curfew. It was scary. Yvonne, who was always the most spiritual of the family, prayed to God to spare her because she did not want to die as a child. During family meals, she was often called on to say the prayer, often short, like the traditional "Bless us, Lord, and bless this meal we are about to eat." During her panic attacks, the prayer began with the *Lord's Prayer* and continued with: "Please, God, I don't want to die. I want to stay alive. I still want to do a lot of things in my life." She could even pray until she was exhausted, just like the day we were all seated with Dad, our eyes closed. We had to open them after a few seconds of silence in the middle of prayer because little miss Yvonne had fallen asleep. We all burst out laughing before finishing the prayer.

Overnight, our bungalow in the garden was transformed into the headquarters (HQ) of the soldiers assigned to our security during Dad's absence. I remember I was always scared to sleep at night because I thought people would come and kill us. Things were better after the body-guards were assigned to our security. They also accompanied us to school and on all our trips.

Dad would still return home occasionally, maybe once every three months. On his second visit, we noticed that he had gained weight. It was no surprise. Dad explained that soldiers ate mainly corned beef in cans and some kind of chocolate protein bars at the frontline. He brought us some from time to time as a gift. I thought it tasted really bad, but knowing it was the only present he could bring us, I didn't say so to him.

The helicopter would land in our yard on a Friday and pick him up on Sunday, sometimes Monday morning. He always seemed tired and worried when he arrived but seemed happy to find his haven of peace, in the middle of nature, in a semblance of calm.

He always started by taking a good, long shower. Then, we heard him sing his famous favorite beatitudes from the parental suite: "Nimwishime munezerwe, kuko ingororano yanyu izaba nyinshi mw'Ijuru." Translation: "Be glad and thankful, for your reward will be great in Heaven." When he was young, Dad had been part of the choir at his sem-inary, so it certainly brought good memories for him when he sang like this during his free time.

Dad loved his weekends to be peaceful. So, no one was told that he was home. The few curious people who had been alerted by the sound of the helicopter landing and who would come and see him in normal times were politely dismissed. He liked to start his day by walking around the property and the garden he was so proud of. He had found plants of all kinds from all over the world. This mix of colors was very relaxing. So, he would spend part of the weekend gardening and making up for lost time.

We took the opportunity to serve all his favorite recipes, such as a good steak with salads and, of course,
pan-browned potatoes or baked plantain gratin, one of
Mom's secret recipes. For dessert, there were fruit salads,
bananas, and milk chocolate (his favorites included Côte
d'Or Original with milk and the Galak milk). Finally, at the
dinner table, he asked us to tell him about our last weeks,
how things were going at school, and more.

In the evening, if he still had the energy for it, we would
sit down to watch a Louis de Funès film. I was dying to
ask him how things were going on the frontline, but I held
back. I imagined he must have seen a lot of horrors. He
told us about a few but took care to ensure we understood
the atrocities that were taking place without describing
anything in detail so as not to frighten us. But he wanted us
to know that outside our golden bubble, there was a whole
other reality in the country, which was taking place at the
same time miles away. At the end, he would invite us to
thank God for His protection.

Prayer helped him overcome the difficulties that came
with his rank and his position as chief of operations in a
zone where death, misery, fear, and violence were the rule.
Although we were spared the details, I would eavesdrop
as he talked about the horror of war. I also listened to the
radio. It was said that atrocities were being committed in
the North. Massacres, beheadings, pregnant women cut in
half, rapes (this is the first time I heard this word which I
found so bizarre that I did not even dare look it up in the
dictionary). There were also reports about the thousands
of displaced people from Nyacyonga crammed into a camp
for internally-displaced people in northern Rwanda who
would soon be camping near our home. Again, I felt a
threat hovering over us.

Whenever Dad returned from the frontlines to spend a few days with us, we found him transformed each time. You could feel it in his way of communicating. He was more patient at times as if he realized that his life was lent to him when he came to spend time with us. He gave thanks to the Lord for being able to be with his family. When he left, he would say his batteries had been recharged for several months.

Dad loved us all and was very proud of us all. He found Maurice, who was then approaching his twenties and had always been very smart, to be like a partner with whom he could talk man-to-man. He, therefore, took advantage of his visits to call Maurice in Europe by satellite. He also sometimes wrote our brother letters describing how things were developing on the ground. He seemed confident that the Rwandan Armed Forces could regain control and find serious foreign partners to help them in the field.

In May, tensions began to rise even at our École belge de Kigali as Rwanda began to return to multipartyism.[2] I remember that one day we learned that some schoolmates had been imprisoned because they were suspected of collaborating with the RPF, the Rwandan Patriotic Front. I remember the image of Pauline, who returned with her hair shaved; she had been detained for a short while. It saddened me. During recess, small groups began forming, relationships became more distant, and the social dynamics weren't the same.

But being in a mixed environment (Rwandans and expatriates), even if we now knew the Hutu/Tutsi meaning, we remained tolerant towards each other. Until then, we had not observed any difference; we spoke the

---

2. Until 1991, the Rwandan political landscape was dominated by a single party, the National Revolutionary Movement for Development (Mouvement révolutionnaire national pour le développement, MRND).

same language and were in the same teenage delusions. Nonetheless, the Kiga/Nduga regional split became more pronounced. The *Bakiga* are people from the North while the *Banyenduga* are from the South. I had friends from all walks of life, be they Hutus, Tutsis, or people from the South or the North. But since Dad was a military leader from the North, we were automatically categorized as close to the government. But this in no way spoiled relations with my best friend Claire, who was from the South, nor did it affect Denise's friendship with Maryse who was also from the South. Quite the contrary!

Maurice brought us some comfort in July by coming to spend the summer with us. Dad was even able to free himself the weekend of his arrival, and we took the opportunity to visit our grandparents.

In the evenings, Dad and Maurice would talk a lot while we went to bed. Dad impressed on Maurice that he did not consider war an option but rather a costly adventure in men and resources for the country. Dad would have preferred to end the war, but he wasn't sure their opponents wanted to. Dad told him very serenely that if peace did not materialize as he wished and he ended up losing his life on the battlefield, Maurice had to be ready to support Mom. His feeling was that the RPF was determined to win the war and wanted to seize power at all costs.

Before returning to Austria, Maurice visited our grandparents one last time in Ruhengeri and Gisenyi. He even brought our two grandmothers together, which was exceptional!

He woke up with the weird feeling that something was going to happen that he couldn't rationally put into words. He just felt he wouldn't return the way he left. To reassure himself, before hitting the road, he still asked our driver

Beaudoin how many years he had had a driver's license. The latter reassured him by telling him that in addition to driving for many years, he had trained in defensive and safe driving, with escape techniques in the event of a trap or ambush. Reassured, Maurice said nothing to Dad or Mom, and they set off in the white Toyota very early in the morning. Maurice was seated on the passenger side. Beaudoin drove very fast, especially passing through the demilitarized zone, which was the buffer zone in north-eastern Rwanda, where the risk of being arrested or killed was greater because of the presence of the RPF. However, the trip had gone without a hitch. He was able to visit our paternal grandmother and our maternal grandparents.

On the way back, it was raining very hard. Maurice was reading. Arriving at the Nyirangarama pass, about fifteen kilometers from Kigali, Maurice suddenly heard Beaudoin say, "*Mana we*" - "My God." He saw the driver panicking. They were on a big bend and the car was losing control. At the same time as he was aware that Beaudoin was trying to take control of the skid, Maurice observed the scene in slow motion, as if time had ground to a halt. He saw his life pass before his eyes—including the stupid things done in his early childhood up to that moment. Maurice experienced what is commonly called a life review, as told by those who have come close to dying, which I experienced a few years later in 1994. He was serene, however, thinking, "What is this? I have only accomplished this (little) in my life?"

Time resumed its normal course. Maurice watched as Beaudoin made things worse by turning the steering wheel in the direction they were skidding. Seconds later, the Toyota veered off the road and flipped over several times as it rolled down the mountain. When the pick-up finally stopped, they were both conscious. Maurice remembered that they had just filled up with gas a few minutes before the accident and since he also had seen several action movies, he knew they had to get out immediately because the vehicle could explode. The villagers began to come running, driven by curiosity. Beaudoin's door was jammed, but Maurice was able to free himself. He went around to get Beaudoin out with the help of another man. Miraculously, both only had scratches. They ran and reached the road where some good Samaritans picked them up and took them to Kigali.

I remember they told us about their accident but I never realized how serious it was. I only remembered that the truck had fallen into a ditch and had to be picked up later.

1992

In Kigali, war was now part of our daily lives. Josiane and Fabrice have very few memories of this period, apart from the heavy atmosphere and the sandbags that piled up in front of the house from time to time. The instability prompted Denise to take an interest in history. Until then, she had never really dwelled on the background of her friends nor on any political considerations whatsoever. Who were these Rwandans attacking their country, and why were there Rwandan refugees in the first place? She would have liked to ask Dad these questions during his quick visits to the house. But one-on-one meetings were very rare, considering the constant presence of our large family and the people visiting us.

One day in February when Dad came by, she wanted to take the opportunity to talk to him alone. That evening, she made sure she was last to bring him the comb for his sacred head massage. After dinner, he really enjoyed clearing the (non-existent) dandruff, *kuvuvura* in Kinyarwanda.

It was always the same ritual. We cleared and cleaned the table and the floor after eating. Even though we had helpers, Mom always told us it was out of the question for others to do it for us! The same rule applied for cleaning our rooms. I can still see her telling me that no one should ever wash my underwear for me! Once the dining room had been "polished," that is to say, cleaned from top to bottom, we tried to sneak away to our rooms to prepare for the night and prepare our school bags and clothes for the next day. At that precise moment, Dad would choose his "victim" among us to come and massage his scalp. Whoever didn't slip away quickly enough, be it Yvonne, Denise, or me, found herself in charge of the task. We all knew he would fall asleep within five minutes, so we went along with it in absolute silence to escape as quickly as possible. Moreover, Denise has inherited the habit. However, since her descendants are less numerous (and also less obedient), she is not as lucky to have her head scratched until falling asleep every evening!

So that day, Denise wanted to keep him awake by asking him to explain to her who the renowned *Inkotanyi* were who had attacked Rwanda. But Dad fell asleep after two minutes. So she had chosen to leave in silence, but she promised to ask the question again when she would have another chance.

The next morning, I too waited for Dad to finish his breakfast to bring up the question I had asked him a few years earlier: what was the difference between *Hutus* and *Tutsis*. I first heard of this ethnic concept at school a few years earlier when I was in primary school. The mystery remained unsolved in my head, but the question aroused an interest, especially in this time of war. Dad took the time to answer me, telling me that there was no difference and that you should never differentiate people, regardless of their background. He stressed that it was important to look at people in an equal and compassionate manner. He said he had loyal *Tutsi* and *Hutu* friends on whom he could count and whom he considered brothers. I will never forget this sentence, which for me is the very essence of open-mindedness: "the enemy of mankind is a man." He added that there are good and bad people everywhere in life and that sometimes the enemy could turn out to be someone very close. That day, he taught me never to judge people by their ethnicity and, by extension, their race, their origin, their skin color, or their religion.

Dad's trips back-and-forth between the combat zone in northern Rwanda and the capital Kigali lasted almost two years. When he was finally able to return to Kigali for good, it must have been in April since it was during the Easter holidays. He was completely transformed by faith. He prayed more and encouraged us to do the same. For Dad, it had to be a way of expressing his gratitude for escaping death on the battlefield. Prayer sustained him in managing his responsibilities and allowed him to handle the pressures he underwent daily. For us children, it was comforting. Seeing him in peace gave us a sense of security.

As for me, I continued my little life as a teenager in a "cool" and rather privileged environment. Our concerns had become basic again and, in a selfish sense, centered on our looks and musical trends coming from other places. We did pretty well at school, and there were pleasant and relaxed classes where we could have a little more fun, like arts and crafts or chemistry. At fifteen, we felt grown up, as if the world belonged to us and we had the whole future ahead of us, despite what was happening.

The EBK sports weekends were legendary. The school was split into the Yellows and the Greens, who sportingly competed in several disciplines. It was a good atmosphere. I was part of the Greens, obviously the strongest. In one discipline, we were unbeatable. It was the shot put. The group consisted of Chantal, Farida, Martine, Patricia, me, and others that I have surely forgotten. The Greens were also the best in track and field, like Anne-Marie or Gisèle, who appeared to run the marathon effortlessly.

Teenage relationships were very genuine in the '90s. We weren't distracted by mobile devices, tablets, or whatever, and we spent time together. We got together at dance parties, the French sports club, the swimming pool, or we organized "pajama parties" with friends.

On Wednesdays, we were allowed to leave school alone. I would come home with friends after a detour to the bakery or the ice cream shop. Often, I went to Claire's. Sometimes with my other best friend, Laurence, who was half Russian, half Rwandan. This always amused me because it was the only time I had heard her speak Kinyarwanda with her father a few years earlier and her accent was worse than mine. Sometimes, Moïse would drop me off at home on a motorbike.

In June 1992, Dad was appointed Chief of Staff of the Rwandan army. Although he was honored to assume command, his responsibilities increased. On one hand, he was responsible for leading the Rwandan army while also shouldering the burden imposed by the dynamics of the extremely expensive war. On the other hand, he had the added challenge of managing a return to peace in a political context of internal divisions.

It was another change for us. In addition to coming back to live full-time with us, he now had to travel with more bodyguards considering his new status and especially the current climate. The same applied for us. We were also assigned an official residence in Kiyovu, in the city center, just across from the presidential residence, where we lived during the week. On weekends, we still returned to Ndera, our main house that was now surrounded by bodyguards. We no longer had much privacy. We now had to be more discreet, limit our movements, or go out under protection. Overnight, our life changed again.

Living in town during the week allowed Dad to attend church daily. There was a thirty-minute mass at Saint-Michel Cathedral that he always attended and took us all with him. It was very early, around seven o'clock in the morning. We went there on foot, a short walk from our residence in Kiyovu. Dad had asked the bodyguards to dress in civilian clothes and to be as discreet as possible. He told us how important it was to respect everyone and never look down on anyone. He often told us that good leads to good. Even if this mass was imposed on us overnight, little by little, we liked to start our days with this moment of communion before going to school.

There were official visits and receptions at home all the time, but our parents preferred to organize them in Ndera since there was more space.

We then hired a chef and waiters who came for an evening. I liked getting involved, being part of the evening coordination, in a way occupying the role of butler or master of ceremonies. My parents let me come and greet our distinguished guests, then I slipped into the bedroom. I liked this period because I felt great and useful, like the elders in *The Sound of Music*, who put on their beautiful outfits while greeting distinguished guests.

For the teenager that I was, seeing the honors and privileges associated with Dad's new status could be overwhelming, but it filled me with pride. With each move, the sirens sounded to let him get by, which impressed us when we were with him. Now people stood up when he walked into a room and the hubbub would give way to silence, especially one day, I accompanied him to the military camp to see his office. Around him reigned such discipline and he received a military salute as he went by. But on weekends in Ndera, he would become an ordinary man again, passing almost unnoticed through the crowd. He ordered the civilian-dressed bodyguards to be as discreet as possible. I was really proud of Dad.

Denise, who had finished her high school education in June, was looking for a direction for the next level of studies. She wanted to go and study in Canada. Still, Dad had chosen the Brussels Management School (ICHEC – Institut Catholique des Hautes Études Commerciales). So, the registration formalities began.

While waiting to leave for Belgium, she took the opportunity to go out with her friends, especially during the weekends. Her outings paled compared to other teenagers who snuck out to go clubbing (in fact, that would have been practically unthinkable at home, as Dad seemed to have eyes everywhere). Most often, this was limited to parties between "grown-ups" who had finished their schooling and were waiting for new adventures abroad. Dad was certainly aware of Denise's few unreported outings. However, he was closing his eyes because he likely realized she was still serious. Dad was like that, watching from afar and letting us fly on our own. We are all grateful to him for that because he taught us to set limits for ourselves within the framework of what we were allowed to do. In July, Denise organized a big house party in Ndera. Maurice returned from Austria in time for her high school graduation evening; it was a bit like *prom night* in the United States.

During that summer, Maurice found the political climate quite tense. He had time to chat with Dad and asked him what his experience of war on the battlefields was, whether he had killed people and if he had seen a lot of deaths ... With great calm, Dad replied that it was a difficult situation. The hardest part was coming face to face with child soldiers. He remained convinced that the cost of the war constituted a hindering of the country's development. He believed that stopping the war was the best solution, although he remained confident that the Rwandan Armed Forces could come out of this as winners. The path negotiated through peace, if it were conducted wisely, seemed to him to be the best option. It would thus have been possible to organize free elections in the context of a multi-party system and set up a national unity government bringing together all the political factions of the moment.

Dad, who had a strong sense of duty, fully supported the discipline required by a military career. Yet he was not a politician, so he was not necessarily a supporter of this or that personality. He was a loyal person who fought for his country.

On October 1, 1992, Dad accompanied Denise to Kigali airport. Neither knew that was the last time they would see each other. It was also for Denise, the last time she would set foot in her motherland for a very long time.

4. The year of hope

I remember 1993 as a really weird year, both euphoric and a harbinger of bad luck. I felt a change in everything as if all our hopes could come true. Denise and Maurice were abroad pursuing their education. So, I was the eldest and took my role very seriously and responsibly. I thought about myself a bit and was very proud of it, like Dad's right hand. He often told me that he appreciated my organizational side; we were very similar in that aspect.

Despite his new duties and being very busy on week-days, he always made it a point of honor to come and have lunch with us as soon as he could free himself. In Rwanda, it was not like in Belgium or in North America. Children went home to have lunch before returning to class in the afternoon. As a result, our friends often said that Dad acted like a Westerner rather than a traditional Rwandan father.

Mom had to take care, in addition to managing her business, of coordinating the many receptions related to Dad's new rank.

Weekends were quieter. We sometimes played board games, our favorite being Monopoly. Or we watched movies when we were not entertaining. Besides comedies and action films, Dad was fond of historical and classic films like *Roots*, *The Longest Day*, and *Conan the Barbarian*. During these moments of relaxation, we often had some chocolate. This is something over which he asserted his authority. It was always the same ritual. Dad opened the box, kept a third for himself, and divided the rest between him and us, not without tasting. In the end, he ate half of the chocolates. Josiane and Denise inherited this love of chocolate and from that point of view, Belgium was defin-itely a good place to be.

Dad remained humble and genuine. People close to him knew he was welcoming and listened attentively throughout his life. Sometimes, we even found that some people abused it. There were, for example, those who always showed up at strategic times at home (for example, at seven o'clock, when dinner was approaching). Our helper Matata informed Dad that such and such was at the gate with a demand. The neighbors also often came with all kinds of requests, from a simple water problem making the road inaccessible to mourning or a lack of money for their children's schooling. Dad always gave what he could. He always had banknotes with him that he gave out.

Whenever he was too busy to meet people, Dad would often ask them to write down their problems, which he took the time to read on weekends. Often, he started his jeep, while we sat in the back seat, and would drive around the neighborhood. On Sundays after mass, he took the time to talk with people and always told us that respecting people of all social classes was important. It was difficult for us to understand at the time, especially for Josiane and Fabrice. They didn't understand this gathering of crowds around Dad.

Insecurity was always part of our lives. We had become accustomed to the sporadic shooting. We even learned to distinguish between the sounds of Kalashnikovs and grenades.

Life went on nonetheless. Socially, we enjoyed our golden youth. I remember many of my friends moving into nice houses. Claire and Alain had moved into two huge villas, and it was nice to spend time with them.

The same year, there was much talk of the "Arusha peace process," whose objective was to end the war started on October 1, 1990, by the Rwandan Patriotic Front against the Rwandan state. Based on Dad's explanations, I also understood that on the military level, these agreements would result in the integration of the RPF army into the Rwandan Armed Forces (FAR) to create a single Rwandan army.

As Chief of Staff, Dad played a key role and took part in formal talks between the two sides to apparently prepare to implement the peace accords.

He continued to free himself to join us for lunch. One day, while we were having lunch in Kiyovu, Dad said to Mom: "Today we met the RPF high command in Mulindi during the military talks. The leader, Major Kagame, told me to greet you." Dad said that the negotiations were progressing well and that if they were successful Paul Kagame would be Deputy Chief of Staff. We took the opportunity to ask him how it would happen and if the war would end. He told us that the Rwanda of tomorrow would unite all Rwandans. He seemed to believe in a renewal. After years of fighting militarily and suffering human losses on all sides, we heard him say that the only viable option would be the unity of the Rwandans.

On the other hand, another day, I remember Dad saying that this same Paul Kagame had told him cynically and, staring into his eyes, that he would take his place. We didn't find it funny at all! But above all, it rekindled a certain anxiety that Dad did his best to calm down. Perhaps the path to peace was not being opened as we had imagined? In private, he confided to Maurice that this made him skeptical about the goodwill of the RPF to emerge from the crisis.

Personally, I was too young to understand the ins and outs. So, all I saw and heard, sometimes behind the doors, was that Dad's hopes were punctuated by worries.

This state of mind is reflected in his personal notes: "*Although thinking that in the camp of the Rwandan Patriotic Front (RPF), there was undoubtedly a desire on the part of some to see the peace agreements succeed; the risk of a resumption of hostilities and particularly an action in the city could not be ruled out.*" Dad, therefore, wondered about "*the RPF's desire to fight as indicated by several signs.*"

On the government side, there seemed to be a real desire to make these agreements a reality. However, Dad was aware of the challenges that awaited them, particularly on the military level, such as *"the logistical question, the concerns about the methods of merging the two armies, the political and socio-economic context, the prevailing insecurity, etc."* It should be noted that *"national security, including the security of Tutsis,"* was at the center of the concerns of the gendarmerie and the Rwandan army.

In the following letter addressed to the President of the Republic on July 28, 1993, Dad underlined that at the military level, the Rwandan Armed Forces (FAR) would hardly resist a new total attack because of insufficient ammunition. Therefore, if that happened, it would be "double or nothing."

Kigali, le 28 juillet 93
Note personnelle au Président de la République

Mon Général,

Le 27 juillet dans l'après-midi, j'ai reçu le lieutenant-colonel Maurin, mon conseiller, qui m'a parlé de la situation qui prévaut à l'ambassade de France à qui Kigali et de celle qui prévaut sur le front.

S'agissant de la situation au sein de son ambassade, il y a lieu de noter l'hostilité de plus en plus ouverte du nouvel ambassadeur envers le régime et en vers les FAR tandis que cet ambassadeur donne plutôt l'impression de flirter avec le MDR, fraction de monsieur Nsegiyaremye.

La dernière fois, quand vous m'avez reçu au village Urugwiro, je vous ai parlé de cette situation. Je me rappelle qu'alors Votre Excellence avait envisagé d'accorder une audience au diplomate français pour dissiper ce climat. Je reste convaincu que cette audience pourrait arranger les choses.

Kigali, 28 July 93
Personal message to the President of the Republic

Dear General,

On July 27 in the afternoon, I spoke with Lieutenant-Colonel Maurin, my adviser, about the situation prevailing at the French Embassy in Kigali and on the battle field. This ambassador gives the impression of flirting with Mr. Nsegiyaremye's MDR political wing, which is notable given the increasing hostility he is showing towards the regime and the FAR.

When you received me in Urugwiro village last time, I discussed this situation with you. As I recall, Your Excellency considered granting an audience to the French diplomat to dispel this climate. It remains my belief that such a meeting would be beneficial.

Permettez-moi à présent d'aborder la situation sur le terrain. Pour commencer et selon les propres termes du lieutenant-colonel Maurin, nous avons évité de justesse un raid ennemi sur Byumba dimanche dernier au moment où à Kinihira, la dernière main venait d'être apportée sur le protocole d'accord. Le FPR a voulu encore nous surprendre car les français, par le biais de leurs écoutes, ont capté la conversation faite alors entre Kagame et Kaka où celui-là disait à celui-ci que les troupes FPR venaient de dépasser les troupes gouvernementales à Byumba.

Let me give you a clear picture of the ground situation. First of all, we barely escaped an enemy raid in Byumba last Sunday, according to Lieutenant-Colonel Maurin. This happened while the finishing touches were made in Kinihira on the protocol of agreement to be

amended. The RPF still wanted to surprise us because the French, through their wiretaps, picked up the conversation then between Kagame and Kaka where the former said to the latter that the RPF troops had just overtaken the government troops in Byumba.

Toute vérification faite, l'on a remarqué que le message disait que les troupes de reconnaissance du FPR « étaient en vue des troupes rwandaises » ce qui montre clairement qu'il y a eu des reconnaissances ennemies en profondeur et des mouvements anormaux de troupes ennemies dans le secteur opérationnel de Byumba notamment à Mukarange (position d'artillerie ennemie) et à Nyabyondo, en face de la commune Cyumba (centre logistique ennemi).

We noticed that the message said that the reconnaissance troops of the RPF "were in sight of the Rwandan troops" which clearly shows that there was deep enemy reconnaissance and abnormal movements of enemy troops in the operational sector of Byumba, particularly in Mukarange (enemy artillery position) and in Nyabyondo, opposite Cyumba commune (enemy logistics center).

D'après le lieutenant-colonel Maurin et d'après l'appréciation qu'a l'état-major de l'armée, nous nous faisons de la situation tactique actuelle, l'attaque ennemie se situera inévitablement autour du 5 août. Elle commencera par Kigali et une tentative d'acharnement ennemie de nos troupes en défensive dans la région de Byumba après un bombardement furieux dans cette dernière ville. À notre niveau, nous avons pris des mesures pour éviter la surprise de la dernière fois et pour poursuivre l'ennemi. Des ordres d'opération ont été déjà donnés au commandement du secteur opérationnel et je crois sincèrement que nos militaires pourraient efficacement faire face, courageusement, à une nouvelle aventure de l'ennemi. Mais, les efforts entrepris sur le plan militaire ne suffisent pas à eux seuls pour arracher une victoire définitive sur le FPR en cas d'une nouvelle agression.

Accordng to Lieutenant-Colonel Maurin and our assessment of the current tactical situation we made with our army authorities, the enemy attack will inevitably take place around August 5. After launching a furious bombing in Byumba, the enemy will attempt to attack our troops in Kigali relentlessly. At our level, we have taken measures to avoid a repeat of the previous surprise and to pursue the enemy. I sincerely believe our soldiers could face a new enemy attack effectively and courageously as orders have already been given to operational sector commanders. Military efforts alone will not suffice to defeat the RPF in the event of a new attack.

En effet :
- Les munitions restent insuffisantes, notamment les bombes pour Mortier 60 mm alors qu'elles sont le plus couramment utilisées. A ce stade, le projet de commande qui devait être fait en Afrique du Sud est bloqué faute de crédit pour payer un acompte de 25%.
- Les véhicules (au moins 7 camionnettes) manquent pour tracter les pièces d'artillerie.
- Aucun plan n'existe, sur le plan de la défense civile, pour canaliser les nombreux déplacés qui campent aux portes de la ville de Kigali.

In fact:
- **Ammunition remains insufficient, in particular 60 mm mortar bombs, which are the most commonly used. At this stage, the purchase order which was to be done in South Africa is blocked for lack of credit**

to pay a deposit of 25%.

- Vehicles (at least 7 vans) are lacking to haul artillery pieces.
- As far as civil defense is concerned, no plan exists for channeling the many internally displaced people to Kigali's gates.

Mon Général, je crois qu'il ne fait pas de doute qu'une nouvelle attaque de l'ennemi va avoir lieu. Ça sera alors quitte ou double. Je propose que vous puissiez réunir encore une fois tous les responsables qui sont concernés par la sécurité de ce pays pour fixer les idées et coordonner les initiatives.

Sur le plan strictement confidentiel, il faut exposer à nos amis français (au plus haut échelon) la situation grave qui peut à tout moment s'abattre sur le pays et leur demander au moins des munitions, surtout les bombes de 60 millimètres, s'ils ne peuvent pas nous donner des troupes.

Telles sont mon Général quelques réflexions que j'avais à vous exposer.

General, I am certain that the enemy will launch a new attack. It will then determine our fate. To coordinate initiatives and set ideas for the future of this country, I suggest you once again bring together all the officials concerned about security.

On a strictly confidential level, it is important that you explain to our French allies (at the highest level) the grave situation that could develop at any time and ask them at least for ammunition, especially 60 millimeter bombs, if they can't supply troops.

Such are, Sir, some reflections which I had to share with you.

Alas, history proved him right.

The Arusha accords were in the final stages of negotiation after talks that had lasted more than a year. Maurice remembers the clause that had been added upon Dad's insistence: Rwanda would not take responsibility for the debts accrued by the RPF. The RPF had received foreign funds to finance the war, partly based on promises to be repaid once in power. But for Dad, there was no question of this debt weighing on the Rwandan state budget.

The final signing of the peace accords took place on August 4, 1993, a historic date full of hope for Rwandans. These agreements provided for establishing democratic and inclusive institutions in Rwanda to achieve lasting peace in the country. In addition, the political and military integration of the various internal and external components of the Rwandan nation represented a hope for a peaceful exit from the crisis which had plagued Rwanda since October 1, 1990.

It was agreed that a battalion of three hundred RPF soldiers would be positioned near the Rwandan Parliament to observe the progress of implementing the Arusha peace accords. However, in his notes, Dad wrote that this number was doubled and that these troops circulated in the capital Kigali at night.

That same summer, Dad kept his promise to send me to Brussels for three weeks in August, after I had received an excellent report card at the end of the school year. This was the first time I traveled alone. Mom gave me a shoulder bag, easier to carry, and entrusted me with a small box with her gold jewelry that my aunt Agnès would get repaired for her and the equivalent of ten thousand Belgian francs (about two hundred and fifty euros) for my stay. Feeling quite mature, I agreed with my uncle Augustin that from Brussels National Airport, I would take a train directly to the central station, about ten minutes away, where he would pick me up by car. Everything went like clockwork except that I forgot my bag on the train, which contained my passport and the small box Mom had entrusted me with. Fortunately, a benefactor found it and returned it intact to the lost and found. Despite this fright, I had an excellent stay with my aunt and uncle, especially braiding my little cousin Sabrina's hair. Never would I have imagined that exactly one year later, in the summer of 1994, fifteen of us would find ourselves crammed into their two-bedroom apartment after fleeing Rwanda!

The second part of the stay was with my sister Denise who lived in student accommodation in Etterbeek. It was obviously a bit more hip at her place, because we went to the cinema or met her friends from the EBK who also lived in Brussels, including Patrick and Fidèle, who died a few years later in Brussels in a car accident. May his soul rest in peace.

My parents had arranged it so that Maurice would pass through Brussels in mid-August and that we could return together to Kigali. Maurice, therefore, returned to Rwanda for the last time. But, he, too, could never have imagined that this was his last vacation in his country. After that, he would never have the chance to visit again.

Back in Kigali, we spent the end of the holidays enjoying good times with family and friends. We remember a few anecdotes with Dad, always gently mocking. In Kinyarwanda, the most appropriate term would be *kunegura*: to criticize but with satire. He did it with such seriousness! He spent his time teasing his niece Béatrice, asking her to put her arm next to his and then with a laugh telling her that she was black as coal!

We remember one evening when a couple of friends were invited to dinner. Dad had, as usual, made sure to receive them well. And as usual, during private events, I was happy to play the matron of the house in place of Mom. They entered the house. Dad took their jackets and invited them to the living room. French doors between the hall and the living room could be opened with a flap in the middle. Half-open, it was less than a hundred centimeters wide. You had to be of average build to get through, no more. As it was not opened often, the flap seemed doomed. The poor lady must have had to pivot to get through the door. The entry of the couple had thus lasted a few minutes. Once our guests were comfortably seated, Dad asked to be excused, claiming to go get the document he had asked me to put away in his office. We went there together because I didn't understand what he was looking for, and to my surprise, he burst out laughing. He then returned to the living room, acting quite naturally.

He also liked to make fun of me, saying that of all his children, I was the luckiest because my late godmother was really kind, generous, and funny. But, on the other hand, her clump of hair did not highlight her hairstyle too much. Indeed, my dear godmother Régine! She was Mom's best friend. She was even her wedding witness. She lived in the Gishwati region of Gisenyi, famous for its *ikivuguto* cow buttermilk. When she came to see us, she brought liters of it and spicy meatballs. It was a party every time she visited. When Régine was there, we no longer saw Mom. We all ate together, they wished us good night, and then settled down together in the living room, where they spent entire nights chatting and laughing while making up for lost time.

The end of the summer was clouded by a car accident, which some have described as an assassination attempt on Dad. He hadn't come home, and we had gone to bed without waiting for him. Mom must have been fretting all night, but we didn't know.

Very early in the morning, a staff car arrived at the house. A soldier had asked to speak to Mom. In a serious but reassuring tone, he told her that Dad had been seriously injured on the road towards our house during the night. His car had rolled over several times in the Nyandungu area, a flat, deserted valley a few kilometers from our home. He had been picked up, unconscious, by a villager who had sounded the alarm.

We had dressed hastily to go to his bedside at the Kanombe military hospital where he had been taken. This same hospital would act as a morgue a few months later, welcoming his corpse and those of his fellow travelers. On entering the hospital, there was a corridor leading to a large room where soldiers were gathered who, according to the explanations we received, had been struck by lightning. That's why in our culture, we don't joke with lightning and always tend to hide when it strikes. Superstition or not, we remember those stories we heard as children of people having their skin peeled off or going blind. We were then told to keep our mouths shut so as not to be struck by lightning! Superstition or not, we always apply this instruction to the letter.

Finally, after long minutes of waiting, we were shown into his room and were all shocked by the sight we saw. Dad had his foot raised and his head completely bandaged. He seemed to be in pain and spoke inaudibly. He could articulate a few words, and then the doctor-surgeon asked us not to linger so as not to tire him further. The doctor then explained that Dad would have surgery on his leg and that screws would be placed to hold his bones together.

At least he was alive! For the first time, we realized that Dad wasn't invincible. Seeing him like this, lying weakened on his hospital bed made us realize that Castar could also give way physically. From that day on, we lived with this feeling and this fear of losing him.

Dad's recovery took a few months. He struggled to regain his physical health and had to undergo painful rehabilitation to walk again. According to Dad, his physio-therapist (who was blind and very skilled) gave him several sessions a week. This therapist had shown us how to help Dad exercise regularly to allow him to regain his mobility more quickly. These were moments of complicity for whoever was responsible for helping him. Watching Dad struggle, day in and day out, enduring the pain was tough but taught us this life lesson to never give up, no matter what. Dad got back on his feet little by little, but his recovery was not complete. He kept a slight limp during his last year of life.

Despite his accident and the rehabilitation that followed, Dad went back to work quickly. Some meetings were held by telephone, and his private secretary often came to bring him papers and have him sign official documents.

The national priority then remained the implementation of the Arusha peace accords. To help implement the agreements, the United Nations Assistance Mission for Rwanda, UNAMIR, was created on October 5, 1993.

"Originally created to help implement the Arusha Peace Accord signed by the Rwandan parties on August 4, 1993. The initial mandate of UNAMIR was to contribute to ensuring the security of the city of Kigali; oversee the ceasefire agreement calling for the delimitation of a new demilitarized zone as well as the definition of other demobilization procedures; oversee general security

Mom, 2021, the day of her 70th birthday.

In training with his peers in the early 1970s. Deogratis Nsabimana, fifth uniformed officer from right.

Déogratias Nsabimana, young officer.

Family photo in Watermael-Boitsfort, from left to right:
Mom, Dad, and our maternal aunt Agnès. In front, from
smallest to tallest: Alice, Denise, and Maurice.

Libya, 1983, Denise holding Yvonne
on her knees and me (standing).

Tripoli, 1983, Dad with Yvonne, during her baptism.

Tripoli, 1983, Aunt Agnès
and Josiane, that same day.

Denise, in Kiyovu, Kigali.

Ruhengeri Market. Dad, in the background,
selecting pieces of goat.

Nkuli, August 1985, Mom and Grandmother Marcianne, Dad's mother, carrying Fabrice.

Our father in the courtyard of his childhood home in Nkuli, chatting with neighbors who came to meet him. I remember an old man who never failed to come by and say hi every time we went to Grandma's.

Mom, her mother, aunt, and father.

My maternal
grandfather
and me.

Josiane, Fabrice,
and Yvonne
in front of our
maternal grand-
parents' house
in Rurembo,
Gisenyi.

Our paternal
grandmother,
in front of her
house with
Josiane and
Fabrice.

Josiane and Fabrice, playing Ninjas in the yard at Ndera.

Mom and Fabrice in Masaka, at Aunt Julienne's.

Moment of a family getaway to Akagera Park, summer 1989; Mom, Alice, Maurice and Josiane, Fabrice and Yvonne.

Denise, Mom, Maurice and the three musketeers in front.

Left to right, Kanyange with arms around Claudine, Josiane, Yvonne, Sabine, and Mom holding Fabrice and Dumu.

Our nephew Maxime and Jean-Paul in the Ndera Bungalow in 2018.

Denise with her classmates at École belge de Kigali.
From the bottom row to the top, left to right: Sylvie K., Sylvie N.,
Denise, Maryse, the late Fidèle, Patrick, Donatien, Edinath.

Dad, on the frontlines.

With our grandparents in
Gisenyi. Uncle Augustin, Dad,
Mom, Josiane, Yvonne, Fabrice
and Maurice on the right.

Maurice and our
late uncle Pacôme.

Fabrice, Maurice, and our late
maternal grandparents.

Before returning to Austria, Maurice visited our grandparents one last
time in Ruhengeri and Gisenyi. He even managed to bring our two
grandmothers together, which was something exceptional!

On the left, our late
paternal grand-
mother Marcianne
Nyirambona, and
on the right, our late
maternal grand-
mother Mélanie
Nyiranuma.

Ndera, February 1992, Mon and Dad in the small
living room during Dad's leave.

Our residence in Kiyovu. Fabrice, Yvonne, Josiane,
and in the middle, Claudine.

One of our distinguished guests, the late Monsignor Vincent
Nsengiyumva, Archbishop of Kigali.

Visiting family at the end of 1992, in Ryinyo. From left to right, front row, Fabrice, Josiane, late cousin Alphonsine, and our late paternal aunt Julienne Kankindi. Back row, our late paternal aunt Généreuse, Grandma, Dad, me, Mom, and our cousin Cyriaque.

Dad in a photo taken at our home sometime after his promotion to Major General.

Grandma and me. It was rare to see her smile. Maybe she knew it was our last time seeing her.

Last photo of dad with his mother. From left to right, Yvonne, Dad, Grandmother, Mom, Margot, Fabrice, and Josiane (kneeling).

Photo of Dad taken after the ceremony to award the medal of Officer of the National Order of the Legion of Honor.

The day he received his medal, before the official reception that followed. Yvonne and (below on the right) I had come home during lunch break. With close family: uncle Athanase and his wife Spéciose, cousin Hilarie and her husband Jean, Dad's cousin, the late Stanislas and his wife, Thérèse.

Decoration, followed by congratulations
by the French Ambassador to Rwanda.

Mom, after congratulating dad. Behind her,
Dad's military adviser, Lieutenant-Colonel Maurin, thanks
to whom our lives would be saved a few weeks later.

I was lucky enough to be present and to be able to congratulate him on my turn.

Photo taken during his acceptance speech.

Dad, General Augustin Ndidiliyimana, Chief of Staff of the Rwandan Gendarmerie, Colonel Luc Marchal and Minister of Defense Augustin Bizimana.

Photos of his personal agenda with pre-noted meetings.

conditions during the final period of the transitional government's mandate until the elections; participate in
demining, and help coordinate humanitarian assistance
activities related to relief operations." [3]

Despite this, at the year's end, the country's situation
was tense. During a conversation that Dad had had with
Maurice, he had hinted to him that the goodwill to share
power and merge both armies (FAR/RPF) was not shared
by the RPF. Dad was also convinced that the RPF had given
its support to the Burundian army in the October 1993
coup attempt, during which Burundi's first democratically
elected president, Melchior Ndadaye, was assassinated.
According to Dad, this showed that the RPF did not have
the will to move towards peace and that Rwanda had to
prepare for the possibility of war resuming.

During the discussions we now had after dinners, Dad
had made it clear to my cousin Didier, who lived with us,
and to me, that there were threats of kidnapping the children of officials. After Yvonne was inadvertently shoved
and pushed to the ground by a man in a supermarket who
had fled before the bodyguard could question him, Dad
had intensified his vigilance. Our outings were now limited, and we were accompanied by bodyguards in civilian
clothes on each trip to avoid attracting attention.

However, the year had ended on a high note in terms of
Dad's military career. He was promoted to major general,
which must have been a great honor for him to achieve one
of the highest ranks as a senior officer. He had received
a phone call. I don't remember who it was. In any case,
he proudly announced to us that he had been promoted.
I remember asking him how many stars he would now

---

3. https://peacekeeping.un.org/sites/default/files/past/unamir.htm

wear and what rank followed. He said there would now be four symbols, with the fifth permanent star representing his "General Staff Brevet" (*Brevet d'état-major* or BEM in French), symbolizing the Command and General Staff Officer training he had attended several years earlier. He then explained that there was still a rung before reaching the supreme rank of marshal, like Mobutu Sese Seko, president of neighboring Zaire. However, I had no doubt that he would make it. Since he had survived the war at the frontlines and a car accident and peace was soon to be sealed, he could reach the highest peak very quickly.

That evening, he let himself dream of the future. He was only forty-eight but had always said that the military retired around fifty. He was making development plans for our residence in Ndera. He talked about Japanese plants he wanted to add to the garden. Part of the land was already used as a vegetable garden, but he saw bigger. Why not thoroughly renovate our second home in Nyakinama, Ruhengeri? He said he and Mom would have a big ceremony for their twenty-fifth wedding anniversary two years later. He added jokingly that he would up the ante for his daughters' dowries to allow them an even more comfortable retirement.

But above all, he had just realized, with Mom, something close to their hearts. They wanted to offer the best gift to children by allowing them to study. So they built the Meldas Institute in Ndera, which welcomed children from primary school and served as a boarding school. Dad even thought of becoming a teacher in his spare time. Both had made it a point of honor to guarantee a certain number of places for poor families.

CHAPTER II

Tipping Point

1. A bittersweet start

Nineteen ninety-four did not start well. Kigali experienced several days of bloody riots in February after the assassination of several political figures, which led to riots and fighting between militias of all stripes.

This is how my school friend, Martine, lost her father, shot dead in front of their gates on February 21. I wrote her a letter of condolences, not knowing that, like her, I would very soon also lose my father. From Brussels, Denise remembers having attended a memorial service for Martine's father and having had a bad feeling. Seeing the sadness of his other daughter Solange and the impact it had on their family, she then wondered what if it was Dad? Unfortunately, she would soon learn what it felt like to lose one's father.

The same month, Dad was awarded by the President of the French Republic the distinction of Officer in the French National Order of the Legion of Honor.[1] It was a huge

---

1. The National Order of the Legion of Honor (French: Ordre national de la Légion d'honneur) is the highest French order of merit, both military and civil. Since its origins, it has rewarded both French and

honor for him. During the official decoration ceremony, he emphasized that the merit was not his alone, expressing his wish "for a lasting peace in Rwanda." He wanted this reward to go to those who fought to achieve peace.

Reading Dad's personal notes up to February 1994,[2] it appears that, as he said in his speech, he firmly believed in peace as the only way out of war. He put his energy into reaching agreements that he believed would last so as to establish new institutions in the country. Therefore, we have chosen to publish them entirely in the appendix so as not to conceal anything and to avoid biasing their interpretation.

Unfortunately, the situation was not improving. On the contrary, the political climate deteriorated sharply in the following weeks.

Yvonne remembers one evening around that time when Dad came home from work. He always had the same ritual. First, he would sit in the living room for a few minutes, drinking a glass of water or a tonic. Then he would shower, and we would all meet at the big table for dinner. That evening at the table he said: "I am very happy because I have achieved what I set to achieve in my life. I wanted to serve my country, and I was able to do so by reaching an honorable stage in my military career." Even though we were in a crisis situation, he seemed happy and serene while pronouncing these words. He was only forty-nine, after all. It's like he had reached that stage in life where we understand that we are on Earth to accomplish a mission, to have a purpose.

---

foreign nationals who have rendered eminent service to France or the ideals it upholds.

2. Please see Appendix I for the transcription and translation of General Nsabimana's personal notes.

Another evening in March, Dad brought my cousin Didier and me together again. We talked for a long time, and he entertained us with amusing stories from his childhood. Dad told us how he walked for miles to go to primary school and that often before leaving he had to fetch water for his mother. He also told us about his time in secondary school and when he went to Rambura secondary school in the neighboring prefecture Gisenyi with his father. They stayed for hours waiting for someone to speak to them. Afterward, a man came out, the cardinal. He looked at them in disdain and said: "I was told that people are waiting for me in this room, but I don't see anyone." So they were treated like less than nothing, which gave him the will to get into this school. He used this example to tell us that we should be masters of our choices. We should never allow ourselves to be intimidated by people who think they are superior enough to dictate our desires. We continued our discussion. He told us that our family was big and that we had to know each other well, and be tolerant of each other.

For the third time, since that episode of primary school where I had asked about the difference between *Hutus* and *Tutsis*, he repeated to us, as he had already done in Ndera, that we should know that "the enemy of mankind is a man." There are bad men everywhere. These words, which he kept repeating, reinforced the humanistic vision my brothers, sisters, and I firmly believe in: never to focus on prejudices or think that one person is better. Applied to the Rwandan context, this meant, and still means, never to demonize an ethnic group because there are good and bad people everywhere.

On March 30, 1994, there was a meeting in Ndera between Colonel Luc Marchal, then deputy commander of UNAMIR, and Dad. By dint of being big and wanting to get involved in everything, there are personalities that I easily recognized. Colonel Marchal later evoked their meeting and Dad's concerns:

"That day, we inspected various tactical positions north of the capital. After this inspection, I asked General Nsabimana for a meeting to inform him of my findings. At the end of the day, I found myself facing a man I felt to be deeply preoccupied. And I can understand that the operationality of this force was cause for fear. What I saw on the tactical positions, which were supposed to counter the axes of progression towards the capital, was a sad sight from a military point of view. By simple conclusion, the units in these positions were incapable of stopping anyone. And certainly not RPF combatants."

Luc Marchal continued: "But that was not the purpose of my visit. I was therefore discussing with the Chief of Staff the distortions observed to the provisions on the weapons containment area. And we mutually agreed on a compliance plan. The subject was exhausted, and the meeting continued as if the general wanted to tell me something else. For a few minutes, we chatted about various things, and like a good Rwandan, he spoke to me about cattle, which shows that we really talked about everything. And then, without concessions, and in a voice tinged with real anxiety, he told me this: 'I fear that the RPF will start the war in the next few days.' Unfortunately, the information available to me left no room for doubt. For several weeks, they have been building up stocks of ammunition and equipment in Uganda along the border. In short, everything you need to support a major military operation (*"opération militaire d'envergure"*)."

"*Envergure*," translated as scope or wingspan, is a term Dad used often ...

Luc Marchal replied that it was "unthinkable. The RPF could not afford such an adventure under the watch of the international community." To that, Dad replied: "The RPF has no use for such considerations. The mistake that you, UNAMIR, are making is to apply to them the same reasoning as yours. But the reality is very different. The Front is a revolutionary movement, and that is how it reasons and sets its own objectives." And Dad concluded: "Against revolutionaries, if you don't adopt the same methods, you will always lose."

Luc Marchal: "I must specify that these words shook me deeply. And that since then, they have not ceased to ring in my ears, and always challenge me with such intensity. Events showed, unfortunately, that General Nsabimana was right."[3]

This meant that since the letter had been sent to the President of the Republic, the operational situation had not changed!

On the eve of the Easter holidays in April 1994, Dad, who seemed particularly preoccupied, brought Didier and me together after dinner. He told us that he had serious information and reliable sources that indicated something was brewing. He was relieved that the school vacation period was beginning. As a soldier, he said he knew that he could have died several times in combat a few years earlier or in an ambush, as he sometimes mentioned, and that his duty included risks. But we sensed then that he feared something would happen to his family. He wouldn't have tolerated that. So he was relieved that we were safe at home for the next few days.

---

3. Source: What Colonel Luc Marchal saw and heard, colloquium of 4/4/2003.

The last time Maurice spoke with Dad by phone was at the beginning of April. Dad told him that he was supposed to come to Brussels and Paris for work meetings and would probably arrive on April 6 or 7. So they agreed that they would meet in Brussels, so they could also see Denise. Dad also told him that many factors indicated that the war could resume at any time, given the activities they had observed in the Demilitarized Zone. According to Dad, the RPF had carried out several incursions, and the indicators clearly showed that the RPF was preparing to launch an all-out offensive. He was almost certain of it. The two unknowns were: When? And what would be the signal that the RPF would use to trigger this general offensive?

Dad remained hopeful that this would not happen. Still, he wanted to warn Maurice that their meeting could be jeopardized should his presence as head of the army be required on the ground if the war were to resume.

He shared the same concern with us in a subtle way. We had heard him say once, from his office, that the army no longer had enough forces to defend the population. Half amused, half worried, Yvonne had asked him if we would be attacked at home. Dad replied that we had to be careful since Rwanda was at war. Yvonne answered saying that if that happened, we could hide under the dining table or under our beds. That day, Dad had also reminded Mom to always have our passports ready and at hand. Mom was already prepared and kept our passports carefully with her little suitcase where she stored her most precious jewels.

2. The attack of April 6, 1994

Monday, April 4

We were in Kiyovu for the Easter holidays.

The morning began with a religious service in Gikondo, which we were to attend as a family. Unfortunately, there were so many people that we could not even enter the church grounds. Dad did not pull his rank to enter. We stood in line for a long time listening to the teachings and songs. Finally, tired of standing and feeling the sweat from the crowd, all of the children (except Fabrice) got back in the car while Dad, Fabrice, and Mom patiently waited for the end of mass.

That evening, before going to sleep, I watched a movie. At the same time, Dad dozed off in the armchair after his usual head massage. I woke him up at the film's end to wish him good night. He told me then that he had learned that day that he was probably going on a mission with the president, but Mom did not know that yet. He asked me not to tell her anything so as not to worry her, given that they were scheduled to leave on April 7 for Belgium. Dad had to do a medical check for his leg and at the same time meet Denise and Maurice, who were to arrive from England.

Tuesday, April 5

During school breaks, we had time to have breakfast all together, depending on who was awake, then Dad went to work. After that, everyone went about their business. Josiane, still very calm, played quietly in her corner with her dolls. She dragged a t-shirt as a comforter, a habit one of her twins seems to have inherited today. Yvonne usually started her neighborhood rounds after breakfast.

At the beginning of the afternoon, Baudoin left to drop off Fabrice at his best friend Dumu's house in Remera. There was also a large field of banana trees around the house, so it was a pleasure to go there and run in the nature playing Ninjas until they were called to come and eat and then sleep. Fabrice reminisces about the rusty sound of the fence that still rings in his ears and the barking of neighborhood dogs.

In the evening, during dinner, Dad received a phone call confirming the mission to Dar-Es-Salaam and the departure details. Back at the table, he informed us that he would leave the next morning to discuss the issues of the Rwandan-Burundian crisis. Mom was offended: "And what about our trip to Belgium scheduled for April 7 then? Deo, can you not postpone your mission until we get back?" Dad calmly replied that it was a day trip and that their plan would not be compromised. He added that the Minister of Defense should have attended. Since he was absent, Dad had to replace him within the framework of signing an additional protocol to the Arusha peace accords. The dinner continued calmly, but the atmosphere had suddenly changed. We could feel Mom grumbling, but she was helpless. She knew that Dad, like a good soldier, had a sense of duty. She could only resign herself to accepting.

I remember that Dad was particularly calm as if he sensed something was going to happen. He stared into space and did not even ask for his head massage session that evening! Josiane and Yvonne went to bed, not suspecting for a second that it was the last time they would speak to Dad and that they would never see him again, at least alive.

While Mom was busy in the bedroom, no doubt finalizing their luggage for Belgium, Didier and I sat down with Dad in the living room for a while. As I wanted to please him, I still took the comb to scratch his nonexistent dandruff. He seemed nostalgic that night. He told us that we had to have our large family's elders meet to talk to us about family history and that he would organize this when he had time. He still told us one or two anecdotes from his childhood. I asked him how his father was. Our generation had never known him. Dad told us that he was small in stature and that he was a very rigorous person. The next day would mark the seventeenth anniversary of Grandfather's death. But the date of April 6 was not necessarily nostalgic for me, given that he had died the year I was born.

Before going to sleep, Dad asked me to go and remind his driver and the bodyguards that he had to leave the house at six in the morning to go to the airport. Coming back, I found him checking to see if the doors were properly closed, as well as the curtains. Then I wished him goodnight, not knowing that this would be the last time I would say goodnight to him.

Wednesday, April 6, the apocalypse

I slept badly, as always when I knew I must wake up early for fear of missing the alarm. I felt that this mission was particularly important to Dad, so I wanted to be on my feet to ensure that the logistics for his departure were ready. Mom knew she could count on me to start the coffee machine.

After a chaotic night, I decided to get out of bed a little before five-thirty. Then I put on my bathrobe. But first, I went to the kitchen to ensure that Matata, our helper, had kept the driver and the bodyguards on schedule. He was already listening to his favorite hymn, which drove us crazy for repeating the same refrain: "*Mbese uwakubaza ikiguzi*

kigura amaraso ye, he, wagikura hehe?" (Where would
you find it if you were asked the price to pay for his blood
[meaning, his life]?) So strong and philosophical when you
think about it!

I went to the dining room to prepare coffee for Dad,
then went back to my room and locked the door before
going back to bed. I could finally sleep peacefully and
sleep in.

I dozed off when I heard Dad knocking on my door.
He knew I had already woken up and just wanted to say
goodbye. I did not even bother to get up, and from my bed,
I said to him: "See you later, Dad. Have a nice trip!" It's as
if a force had confined me to bed. He thanked me for the
coffee and said, "See you tonight!" Then, for the last time,
I heard his voice and footsteps moving away down the hall
to join Mom in the living room. If I had known that was
the last time I would hear from him and see him, I would
have taken the trouble to stand up and tell him that I loved
him and was proud of him. This will always remain among
the greatest regrets of my life.

For Josiane, the day started with breakfast. Then, like
the wise and independent little girl she was, she went about
her business in her corner, cuddly toy t-shirt in hand, since
Fabrice was not there to play with her.

As for Yvonne, she followed her routine that day, and
Mom did not even worry about it anymore. When she
woke up, Dad was already gone. After quickly swallowing
her breakfast, Yvonne rushed out to spend her day having
fun. She remembers seeing practically all the friends in
our neighborhood that she knew like the back of her hand!
In the morning, Yvonne visited those on the south side
of our Kiyovu neighborhood. Despite the insecurity she
experienced on leaving our residential area protected by

our bodyguards, she went there. She passed by the Saint-Michel Cathedral to see, among other things, her friend Nadia's new home, where she spent the rest of the morning.

After spending a few days with friends in London, Maurice arrived in Brussels on April 6 in the morning. He had not spoken to Dad since their last conversation the week before when they had arranged to meet in Brussels. So, upon arriving, Maurice went straight to our aunt Agnès and our uncle Augustin's home. They told him that Dad had told them by phone the night before that plans had changed as he was to fly to Dar-Es-Salaam, Tanzania, and return on April 6. So the trip to Europe would take place somewhere from April 7 or later in the week if nothing else unforeseen happened. Maurice slept for much of the day, recovering from his overnight journey. Then he spent the rest of the evening quietly, waiting for Denise who was to join them later.

I remember the atmosphere at home was very weird that day in Kiyovu. During lunchtime, there was a power outage, so Matata prepared a salad for us, which was to be accompanied by fries he wanted to cook on a hot plate. The power from the backup generator was probably not strong enough because they failed to cook properly. So we settled for bread to go along with the salad. Yvonne came home for lunch and left immediately afterward.

Mom came back from the store in the early afternoon, particularly upset. She blamed Matata and Cyrille, our helper from Ndera, for not cleaning up properly. Cyrille had come to help clean the Kiyovu residence since it was very large. She thought there was a strong smell of rotten meat in the house! As hyperactive as she was (and still is, by the way), she took a mop and started cleaning the hall-way leading to the bedrooms and the master suite, saying she could not stand the stench. A stench that we could not smell.

It rained heavily that day. In the afternoon, I remember seeing Baudoin busy in the garage. He had accompanied Dad to Kanombe international airport in the morning. He told us that they went through such thick fog on the way to the airport that it stopped them dead on the road. Beaudoin asked Dad if they should not turn around instead, as it seemed impossible to cross. Still, Dad refused, insisting on the importance of his presence on the mission. Finally, he said to him, "Go for it."

A little later, I argued with Didier because we both wanted to accompany Baudoin to pick up Dad at the airport in the late afternoon. Yet only one seat was available as two bodyguards had to be present, one in the back and the other in front. Protocol demanded that no one be in the middle, and there was no getting around it. So to avoid making anyone jealous, even if I secretly felt I was the most legitimate to go there, we decided that no one would go. I had always got on very well with Didier, and I liked the idea of having the equivalent of a brother of my generation at home. So I preferred not to come into conflict with him.

Yvonne reappeared at the end of the afternoon. Often worried that something might happen to Dad since his accident in Kanombe the previous year, she would call him on his direct line at the Army Headquarters when he came home late. Unfortunately, that day, unable to call him anywhere (cell phones did not yet exist in Rwanda), her first question was to ask if Dad had given any sign of life.

After showering, we got ready for the evening. Around seven o'clock, we set the table for dinner. We started with our little prayer ritual, then ate, leaving Dad's plate there since he was supposed to come at any moment. Then we sat in the living room to watch a movie.

Denise had the same idea in Brussels since she scheduled a movie night. So, with her friend Assumpta, they went to see the film *Philadelphia*. Maurice, meanwhile, spent a quiet evening at our uncle's. They were waiting for Denise to arrive later that evening.

In 1994, technology did not yet allow the public to follow high-profile meetings in real-time as is done today, nor to instantly tweet about their concluding remarks. Instead, we would only read the following later:

> Letter from the acting Chargé d'Affaires addressed to the Secretary-General of the Permanent Mission of the United Republic of Tanzania to the United Nations, transmitting a communiqué issued during the regional summit meeting held in Dar-Es-Salaam on April 6, 1994. S/1994/406, April 7, 1994.

> Point 7: Regarding Rwanda, the leaders noted with concern that all the transitional institutions that were to be set up after the signing of the Arusha Peace Accord on August 4, 1993, were not yet fully in place. In this regard, they urged all parties concerned to respect the letter and the spirit of the Arusha Peace Accords and, in particular, to establish all the remaining transitional institutions without further delay.

> Done in Dar-Es-Salaam, April 6, 1994

It was around eight-thirty, and we had just started *The Sound of Music* when a deafening noise rang. We were all shaken up. Mom yelled at us to turn off the volume. This time, it was different from the sounds we were used to. This one was louder, a kind of "one-shot" followed by silence. A few seconds later, we heard the same explosion, more noticeable this time. It was terrifying. We ran out of the living room and arrived at the terrace. We saw the light in the sky from afar as if it were fireworks. But was it really fire? Impossible to say. Looking in all directions in the garden, our bodyguards ordered us to return to barricade ourselves inside and lie on the ground while they investigated what had just happened. We heard them screaming. Some said, "the Boss has not even come home yet."

As soon as we returned to the living room, our two phones started ringing simultaneously and nonstop! Mom, who had a bad feeling, told us at first not to answer. But with the incessant phone calls, we resolved to divide the lines between us. So Mom answered the internal army line, and I answered the external line. "Where is the Chief of Staff? This is a crisis situation," they shouted from the other end of the line. We tried to explain everything we knew. The Chief of Staff was away. It seemed like chaos, but we still had no idea what had just happened.

There was a similar effervescence in Brussels at our uncle and aunt's apartment. After dinner, the phone rang. Commander Gijsbrechts, a friend and colleague of Dad's since the 1970s, had just called and asked to speak to Maurice. Gijsbrechts was then military adviser to the Belgian Minister of Foreign Affairs and in charge of military-technical cooperation. He said, "Maurice, do you know where your father is? I cannot reach him, and we have a problem." There was apparently a military plane en route to deliver supplies for the Belgian contingent of UNAMIR. But unfortunately, the plane could not land because the control tower had advised them to change their route since another plane, also due to land in Kanombe, had just crashed. So, Maurice told him he would try to reach Dad and get back to him when he had more news. So, he phoned Kigali directly and got Mom on the phone. It was probably during the minutes following the plane crash because we did not yet have exact information on what had just happened. How could we have imagined for a moment that the plane carrying Dad back had just been shot down while it was landing?

Maurice then tried his luck with the Army HQ. He remembers briefly reaching Major Ntirikina on the phone, who was unaware of the situation. After that, Maurice called Commander Gijsbrechts back to report that Dad had not yet returned from his trip to Dar-Es-Salaam with President Habyarimana that morning.

For my part, I remember that the first person I spoke to was Mr. Mbonampeka. He was the first to tell us that, from reliable sources, the presidential plane had been shot down and asked where Dad was because rumors said that he was also on board and that there were no survivors. I felt my blood turn cold and overwhelmed. So the plane was shot down, no survivors. Besides a lump in my stomach, I no longer remember what I answered or if I hung up on him without saying a word.

The flurry of phone calls continued for a few long minutes, sometimes from friends asking where Dad was, sometimes from officials wanting to speak to the Chief of Staff. It seemed unreal as if we were spectators and actors in a bad movie. We would have liked for time to stop.

At the same time, in Brussels, Maurice and our uncle Augustin were constantly placing phone calls to Kigali between our house and the Army HQ. Uncertainty reigned. Which plane had crashed? The only precise information that Maurice had received and that he had relayed to Commander Gijsbrechts was that two planes had taken off in the morning from Kigali in the direction of Dar-Es-Salaam.

After barely ten minutes, which seemed endless, we had the president's residence on the line. It was Jeanne,

President Habyarimana's eldest daughter. She wanted to be reassuring. She asked us to keep hope because there were two planes, and it was unclear yet who was onboard the one that had just been shot down. Yvonne and Didier circled around the living room, looking at us without understanding what was happening. We sent the two youngest, Josiane and Claudine, to bed, promising to wake them up as soon as there was more information.

In Brussels, Commander Gijsbrechts had apparently gathered more details since he communicated to Maurice that, according to reliable sources, President Habyarimana's plane, which had a particular sound signature that people had recognized, had just been shot down. But, just as Jeanne told us almost at the same time, the identity of the victims was not yet known.

Around 8:50 p.m., the president's wife, Mrs. Agathe Habyarimana, ended all our hopes. Based on the mangled bodies scattered in their garden, there was unfortunately no longer any possible doubt. In a sad voice, she courageously announced to Mom that it was all over, that they had just lost their husbands and that there were no survivors among the twelve passengers on board the presidential Falcon. She added that we needed to be strong and pray for the deceased. Mom remained very dignified. She called Brussels directly to notify Maurice, our aunt, and uncle, that everyone was dead. They had also anxiously waited, while praying that Dad had taken the other plane. Mom also called Dumu's family, where Fabrice had spent the night. Everywhere in Kigali, everyone had obviously heard the same thundering sounds. Mom told them the news. Edinath, Dumu's mom, and Steve, the big brother, decided not to tell Fabrice anything and would wait for Mom to do so the next morning when we went to pick him up on the way to see the corpses. How does one tell a nine-year-old child that his father has just died in a plane crash?

The news was so brutal that it took us time to recover from the shock. Each of us had a different reaction. Claudine was sleeping peacefully. Josiane recalls that when she woke up and heard the news, she was so shocked that she first giggled nervously to take in what was being said to her. Yvonne, meanwhile, cried a lot until she fainted. Then she began to pray. Yvonne implored God to spare our family and prayed for our safety. She added that she did not want to die. Poor Didier seemed petrified. He kept repeating: "It's not possible, not you, Uncle. Not you. Why you? Why are you abandoning us?"

At that very moment, I remembered those horror stories we had heard about how the RPF killed people in war zones. Would the same thing happen to us since Dad was no longer there to protect us? What would become of us?

In Brussels, Denise, whose voice was shaking when she recorded this story, heard the news brutally. At the movie's end, she and her friend took the metro to a station where they could get out and then take a connecting streetcar to Uncle Augustin and Aunt Agnès' house. Instead, they saw a Rwandan student, Fabienne, at the streetcar stop, who immediately walked towards them. Her grave and serious air contrasted with the levity and carelessness of Denise and her friend, who were busy laughing out loud. Fabienne said, "Ah, but Denise, do you not know what happened?" Denise replied no, of course. Then, Fabienne told her point blank: "The president's plane was shot down, and your father was on board; all occupants were killed."

Denise then rushed off in search of a phone booth. She called Aunt Agnès, who handed the receiver directly to Maurice. He told her they were looking for her, that she had to come immediately. Maurice, who was himself in shock, preferred to spare her the details, which he himself had such a hard time digesting.

The 'aftermath' began at that moment. That morning, we were carefree, far from imagining that our destiny would be sealed on April 6, 1994, at eight-thirty in the evening. We lost track of time. Everything had happened so quickly.

Around nine o'clock, we still did not measure the extent of what had happened less than an hour earlier. Major Baransaritse, a forensic doctor, confirmed by telephone that the soldiers were busy collecting the remains of the bodies in the presidential residence of Kanombe because the plane had fallen near the swimming pool.

My pragmatism immediately took over. I dried my tears and then began to think, naively, that the rest would unfold traditionally. We would retrieve Dad's body, prepare for the mourning at home, the funeral service booklet, the suit that Dad would wear for his burial, burying, and trying to get back to normal life. Unable to remain confined to the hallway any longer, I started by comforting Didier, who was still crying. Josiane and Yvonne were asleep. Out of the corner of my eye, I watched Mom. She seemed completely dejected and exhausted. She had taken the phone back to the hallway and was sitting on the floor, her eyes wide, as if hoping for a call from Dad who would tell her that it was a bad joke and that the next day, they would take the flight to Brussels as planned.

There was chaos in the house. We were all very scared and beginning to understand that this attack would create upheaval in the country, with many important figures simultaneously dead on the plane. We felt like we were living in a nightmare. We tried to find out more, but the bodyguards prevented us from leaving, ordering us to regroup in the hallway, which was the least visible part of the house. As for them, they seemed not to know what to do, as if they were waiting for Dad to come back to give them instructions.

As a good organizer, I went to the master suite and emptied the cupboards of Dad's things. Still in shock and trying to figure out what was happening to us, Mom tried to talk me out of doing this task, thinking it was not the right time. I did not listen to her and started by taking out the suits, making two piles, one for Maurice and the other to give away. I then took out the shirts. I remember thinking to myself that there were some very nice ones, a Dior, that I particularly liked. I thought that Fabrice would like it when he was older. There were also some shirt jackets that Zairians/Congolese called *abacost* ("down with suits") that Dad wore when he went on a mission to Zaire. It was probably my way of occupying my mind and coping with the shock.

After that, I went back to the hallway with the others. Mom, Didier, and I did not sleep all night. All the feelings were mixed, from sadness, incomprehension, anguish, fear to anger. We stayed cloistered there, glued to each other, trying not to make a sound, unable to speak or think of anything. Impossible to make sense of it all. Again, we felt the need to pray. We repeated the Lord's Prayer over and over.

For those who were in Brussels, the night was also very long. The news of the attack spread like wildfire within the community. Many Rwandans began to flock to my uncle and aunt's apartment. Like my parents when they lived in Brussels in the '80s, many students considered Uncle Augustin and Aunt Agnès moral figures. *Gutabara* (literally lending a hand to the bereaved) is very important among Rwandans. The mourning began naturally. Maurice came from time to time to greet the people who gathered in the living room, then returned to the bedroom. Not having come especially for him, those who recognized him were all the more moved and offered their sincere condolences. And that sounded odd in his ears, given that he had arrived in Brussels in the morning expecting to see Dad and Mom the next day.

Denise also arrived, finding many people already in the living room. She had learned the news so brutally that a black hole enveloped her that evening. She does not remember anything till the next day.

3. The outburst

April 7

We turned on the Rwandan public radio around five o'clock in the morning, and the station was broadcasting classical music on a loop, synonymous with national mourning. The journalists repeated the same message: President Habyarimana's plane returning from a peace mission in Dar-Es-Salaam had been shot down on April 6 at 8.30 p.m. on its final approach to Kigali airport. They read out the names of the passengers who had perished on board:

The Rwandan delegation:
- President Juvénal Habyarimana;
- The Chief of Staff of the Rwandan army, Major General Déogratias Nsabimana;
- Ambassador Juvénal Renzaho;
- Colonel Elie Sagatwa;
- Doctor Emmanuel Akingeneye;
- Major Thaddée Bagaragaza.

The Burundian delegation:
- President Cyprien Ntaryamira;
- Minister Bernard Ciza;
- Minister Cyriaque Simbizi.

The French crew:
- The pilot, Jacky Héraud;
- The co-pilot, Jean-Pierre Minaberry;
- The flight engineer, Jean-Michel Perrine.

It was the first time that I heard that the president of Burundi and two of his ministers were also on board. The newscasters also said that the authorities urged the population to remain calm and stay home. A bit like now, as I write these lines, during this period of confinement due to Covid-19!

A convoy of three armored jeeps escorted by soldiers and the presidential guard came to pick us up around seven in the morning so that we could gather near our dearly departed at the president's residence in Kanombe, where the plane had crashed.

On the way, Mom insisted that we pick up Fabrice. He was already set to go, and a few minutes later, Steve and his mom brought him to the middle jeep, where we were sitting. I could not help but shed tears when I saw him get in. We were all becoming orphans, but he was our youngest, "Daddy," Dad's little Ninja, who suddenly found himself without his hero. I reckoned that at seventeen, I had at least had the chance to have known Dad better and that it was too unfair for Fabrice at only nine years old.

He was surprised that everyone had come just to pick him up. He did not understand why everyone was calm. Fabrice sensed that something unusual had happened. He told us that his morning had not gone as he liked. They had been woken up early to eat breakfast. He thought everyone was weird, even Aunt Edinath and Steve, who were already up and listening to "sad" music on the radio. He ate bread with hot milk. Then he was told to get ready because Mom was on her way to pick him up. He was disappointed to have to leave so early as he had planned to play all day with Dumu.

Once he got into the jeep, Mom took his hand and told him that something terrible had happened to Dad. A plane crash. And that Dad was dead. Fabrice asked if he was in heaven. Mom told him we would see Dad's body where he died with others, but Dad would not see or hear him. Fabrice nodded quietly, no doubt trying to absorb this information. Then he fell asleep on Mom's lap.

On the way to Kanombe, the landscape passed before our eyes. In the past, I liked this road because we used it on weekends, with Dad driving, when we returned to Ndera. But I could not see anything. I was lost in thought, staring into space. On the way, we heard gunshots. We could smell plastic from burnt tires and felt like we were watching a bad movie.

Arriving at the president's residence in Kanombe, many vehicles were already parked in the driveway. I immediately noticed that the fence was half destroyed. We were led straight to the living room, where horror awaited us. There was a dead silence, sometimes punctuated by a few barely audible cries. Rwandans are discreet by nature. I realized this when I once attended a Congolese mourning, where people were almost rolling on the ground screaming. As I learned later, some cultures even invite professional mourners during times of grief.

The bodies were lying in the middle of the large living room, side by side. All were covered in white blankets or sheets, some marked with bloodstains.

WARNING, some images may upset the youngest and most sensitive people.

(Photos taken by Jean-Luc, President Habyarimana's son, a few minutes after the crash of the Falcon 50 and on the morning of April 7, 1994. With the author's agreement, we have chosen to publish some of them.)

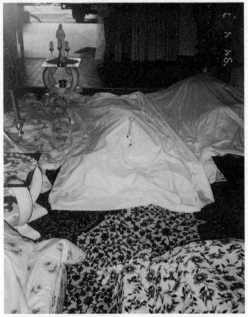

The bodies lying in the living room,
our first glance at our fathers, April 7, 1994.

I recognized a few widows, children of Dad's traveling companions, and other people close to the families.

Fabrice remembers a lady who took his hand to show him Dad's body. She was one of the nuns, President Habyarimana's older sister. We all went to see him at the same time. Slowly and delicately, a soldier lifted the covers to show us. They had been able to gather what they thought were his remains. Josiane was outside when we were shown his body, so she believed for a long time that Dad was not dead and would reappear! The same was done for each deceased; each family present had the opportunity to see their loved one (or what was left of them) lying on the ground. The same lady told Fabrice, Josiane, and Yvonne: "Your Dad died on the plane, and you can not see his whole body because he cut himself in two in an attempt to jump." No doubt she wanted to protect their susceptibility. We have often heard this so-called version which we think is far-fetched. Imagine the scene of someone trying to jump out of a plane between two missile shots! Did we want to push the Castar myth as far as it would go?

Dad's face tilted slightly to the side, was almost intact, recognizable, and expressive. He seemed to be sleeping peacefully. His eyebrows were well drawn. You could clearly see the line in the middle of his eyebrows, which only people who were used to observing him closely knew. However, the length was not there. Lying like this, it looked like the body of a child. We only saw the torso. The legs must have been sideways, jagged. Dad, whom I had spoken to the morning of April 6, was lying there in pieces. It was impossible to believe that he could not speak or hear us. Fabrice remembers having felt sadness, but he was unable to cry. I felt like someone was hitting my head with a hammer, and I was gasping for air. I wanted to get out of this room as soon as possible. Along the way, I also had the strength to look at the body of President Habyarimana, who had lost half of his face, the other half remaining intact.

Outside, the spectacle was even more distressing. The presidential guard members gave us a military salute as a sign of respect. I felt my blood turn to ice. The scene was one of absolute horror, pure butchery. At least in the living room, the bodies of our fathers were neatly gathered and lying. The garden was still in its rough state. You could see the brick wall completely destroyed by the plane's wreckage. The green space, once magnificent, had completely changed color. There were pieces of fresh flesh, teeth, intestines, and so on everywhere. I'll never forget the smell of fresh flesh, even less breathable than in the living room. I remember a plastic sheet that was filled with blood.

Then, I saw Jean-Luc Habyarimana, who is from my generation. After briefly hugging us, he told Irené Akingeneye and me that he had been swimming with his cousins in the pool the night before, pointing to it. It was now covered in blood. They had waited for his father to come home to get out of the water and go eat. Jean-Luc had recognized the sound of his father's Falcon. Just as they were about to leave, a detonation sounded, followed by another a few seconds later, then an explosion. It all happened very quickly. The events and what he had just experienced had no doubt aged him prematurely. We could imagine the violence of the shock through his narrative. However, I found him very brave. He suddenly seemed like an adult, no longer a teenager. We consoled each other by saying that at least our fathers probably did not have time to be afraid, realize what was happening to them, or even suffer.

We went back inside, to the living room, like automatons. It was too much information for our brains to take in at once. But it was better than being in the garden. A few people came in and offered their condolences and then left immediately. Inside the presidential residence, the phone occasionally rang, interrupting the prayers, the only thing we could devote ourselves to. A little later, a soldier approached Mom and told her that they had found Dad's wallet intact in his inside pocket. It contained the equivalent of seventy-five thousand Rwandan francs (or just under five hundred euros). I know that Dad had this money for his trip to Belgium scheduled for the next day, and no doubt he would have liked to exchange it for Belgian francs when they arrived in Brussels. We will never know, but as usual, God does things well because that money helped us a few days later during our escape.

It was too sad to stay in the living room among the corpses and the stench, which kept getting stronger. A lady first led us to the kitchen, where we drank water and ate cookies. Then, we went upstairs with the youngsters and the Habyarimana cousins. Finally, I remember being able to sleep for the first time since the day before.

On the same day, Maurice was busy looking for plane tickets so Denise and he could come to Kigali on Thursday, April 8 or Friday the 9th. At that point, the situation was such that flights still seemed possible. I remember feeling relieved the morning before we left to see the bodies at President Habyarimana's when Maurice informed us on the phone that they were coming. So much responsibility weighed on my shoulders, given that I was the eldest sibling at home at that time. Before hanging up, Aunt Agnès and Denise asked us for our exact sizes so they could buy us black outfits to wear at the funeral. They were thinking of white shirts, black jackets, and skirts for the girls, and a black suit for Fabrice. For Mom, they would look for *umukenyero,* the traditional Rwandan outfit once they arrived in Kigali.

Next, Maurice contacted the Austrian scholarship office in charge of foreign students at his university in Graz. Still unaware of how the situation would deteriorate, he asked permission to miss class for a few days. He explained that his father had just lost his life in the attack on the presidential plane. They were very understanding and even offered to help him buy his return ticket to Kigali.

Maurice remembers that the situation deteriorated very quickly. Our little "land of a thousand hills" was becoming infamous and making headlines on TV. They spent the rest of the day glued to the television, following the distressing news from Rwanda.

April 8

We spent the night, several of us crammed into a room. We were so emotionally tired that we did not mind any discomfort. When we woke up, going down to the living room, we found our mothers sitting in the same place. I do not know if they had any time to sleep. They were there, staring into space, mute. We prayed in the living room, then went back to the bedrooms. The stench had become unbearable and, for me, unbreathable. I did not have the courage or the desire to venture into the garden. It might have already been cleaned up, but I could not bear to see those bits of flesh again.

In the afternoon, when we came downstairs, Jeanne Habyarimana was on the phone trying to organize the transport of the bodies to the morgue. We heard that the situation was explosive, and that fighting was underway in Kigali. Everyone was afraid.

My uncle Stanislas, Dad's paternal cousin, brought us eggs in the evening. Even though we were not focused on food, and no one really thought about it, we realized we were starving as we ate up his freshly collected eggs from his farm.

In Brussels, the bad news continued to stream in. Denise, Maurice, and Aunt Agnes' family could not reach us. They certainly knew that we had gone to Kanombe, but they did not know when we would return to our residence in Kiyovu. There were no cell phones yet, so there were no instant means of communication. Moreover, the telephone lines were apparently unstable. So, to kill time, they started preparing for the funeral.

People continued to gather at my uncle and aunt's. Among the friends who came to support them morally that day were Marcel and Juliette, the children of Mr. Kavaruganda, Chief Justice of the Rwandan Supreme Court. Maurice, who shed tears as I recorded this passage with him, said they had come willingly to associate with them in pain. But, being there, they had also just learned that their father had been assassinated by the presidential guard after the attack, likely in retaliation. So, it was a rather paradoxical situation: they were in solidarity with each other in the face of the drama that our country was going through, and they were there to hug each other and exchange condolences, crying together.

April 9

We spent this third day since Dad's death in Kanombe, a day similar to the day before. The only difference is that the smell of corpses was beginning to be felt everywhere in the presidential villa. That afternoon we attempted to transport the bodies to the morgue. A failed attempt.

There were too many shots. The soldiers told us we had to wait because we risked falling into an RPF ambush. These same soldiers said that the elements of the RPF had left the Rwandan National Assembly (Conseil national du développement CND), where they were consigned under the Arusha accords, to launch a military offensive in Kigali. We well imagined our fate if such had been the case and had we fallen into their hands.

We did not want to take any risks. We resigned ourselves to spending the night at the president's residence, piled on top of each other, mixing prayers and tears while evoking the memories of our fathers suddenly torn from life.

CHAPTER III

The Exodus

1. Uncertainty and preparing for grief

April 10

In the morning, we finally managed to leave under good escort, in convoy, with all the bodies headed for the morgue of the Kanombe military camp near the presidential residence.

Upon entering the building, several bodies were stored. For some corpses, the blood looked still fresh. I have never seen so many corpses in my life. But after seeing the shriveled bodies of our fathers, I was not affected seeing those who were at least dignified because they were whole with their arms and legs.

We were directed to a tiny room, presumably intended for dignitaries (VIPs), where only two bodies could be deposited. Therefore, those of the two presidents, Habyarimana and Ntaryamira, were chosen based on protocol. Next was a larger room where the other bodies could be placed. I no longer remember if those of the French crew were still in Kigali or had already been repatriated to France. Just as I no longer remember what happened to the

Burundians. It all only took a few minutes. We were told
that the corpses would remain there while preparations
were made for a state funeral. First, they would be placed in
cold rooms to avoid rapid decomposition of what was left of
them. Then, when the time came, they would be taken out
of there and prepared for the state funeral. It was the last
time we saw them because that funeral never took place,
nor any other farewell ceremony for that matter. Sadly, we
never saw them again.

We walked along a corridor to cross another room with
other corpses as we left. I was very moved to see the body
of a lady in the middle of all the corpses of the soldiers. She
was beautiful, she had curly hair. Fair-skinned, she was
dressed in black and white. I thought I recognized in her
the person of the Prime Minister, Agathe Uwilingiyimana,
having seen her sometimes on television. Later, we heard
about her assassination, as well as the assassination of ten
Belgian U.N. peacekeepers, which occurred on April 7.
So, it was really her that I had seen. May she rest in peace.
More poor orphans. They lost their mother. It's not that
one parent is more important than the other, but I always
thought Dads died before Moms. Being a teenager, I found
Mom too demanding, considering she could not stand
idleness. Yet we all knew that she was our "Minister of the
Interior," who managed the house daily with a masterful
hand. Dad had the "easy" role because he only intervened
when things got complicated.

We returned to Kanombe under heavy escort. Having
no more reason to stay at the president's residence, we took
the road to return to our residence in Kiyovu. We were
warned that we should follow detours to reach the city to
avoid an RPF ambush. This only fueled our fears. How
long would we be able to keep the second home now that

Dad was dead? My pragmatic side took over, and my fears too. I told myself that a new Chief of Staff would soon be appointed and that we would find ourselves confined to Ndera. Just the idea of no longer having bodyguards to ensure our protection scared me, especially in a future that was becoming more uncertain.

The trip back to the house felt endless. The streets bore witness to the reigning chaos. Our military escort had ordered us to keep our heads down for safety and not look outside. But I remember I still wanted to look through my fingers. Every time I did, I saw bodies and burning tires. We went through many roadblocks of Interahamwe militia men but given our escort, we had no trouble reaching Kiyovu.

People were everywhere in the house. My aunts, uncles, and a few cousins, who had come to mourn with us, had arrived gradually. Everyone seemed lost, wondering what was going to happen. Mapengu, a Tutsi and very good friend of Dad's, was also there. He had spent last Christmas Eve with us. He often came to our house, and I liked it when he was there because we often ate skewers and could drink Fanta, like every time we had guests. He was sad and seemed scared. Mom thanked him for being there and told him he could stay with us as long as he wanted, which he did with relief.

In the afternoon, the apparent calm outside, at least in the neighborhood, contrasted with the hubbub of the house. We called Brussels to share news and find out when Maurice and Denise would arrive. Maurice told Mom that Rwanda's situation was rapidly deteriorating and that we had to prepare to leave the city. He added that he was looking for a solution to get us out of the country. According to what was reported on the news, Rwanda was clearly approaching an apocalyptic situation. There was talk of militias organizing political assassinations in retaliation for the president's death. Furthermore, Commander Gijsbrechts had informed Maurice that the RPF had launched an offensive and was organizing killings around the Rwandan National Assembly, the CND, and that we had to get out of Rwanda. They were looking for a way to get us out of Kigali.

We spent one night in Kiyovu, trying to sleep as best we could. There were so many people everywhere.

April 11

The next morning, I tried reconnecting with the outside world to follow what was happening. Since I was not following the news, we were not really aware of the extent of the drama unfolding around us. We were also trying, as best we could, to grasp what was happening to our family, which had just been beheaded of its leader and patriarch.

We received some very bad news. I spoke with some school friends from École belge de Kigali, and they informed me of the death of some of our friends, like Malaïka and Marie-Aimée. Some families were massacred, like Kiko and Corneille's, and others in the Remera district. Later, my dearest Liliane and Janvier, a friend from EBK, would suffer the same fate. I do not remember the exact timeline. It was said that the families of some had been assassinated by soldiers of the Rwandan army, others by Interahamwe militiamen, and still others had perished under the bullets of the RPF. No matter who killed them, I felt great sadness for all those families because I understood what they were going through. In addition, it was shocking to learn of the death of friends or their families, whom I had seen a few days earlier at the coffee shop of the Belgian school. It was unfathomable at our age and still is today.

Then I tried to call Jeanne Habyarimana to check if they were still in Kanombe, but I could not reach her. I was well aware that we were a family at risk. I remembered what Dad had told us a few days earlier. He was afraid that the children of key officials would be taken hostage by the RPF. Meanwhile, Mom and the rest of the family were busy praying and planning the logistics of the funeral that would be held in Ruhengeri in the days to come.

An incident took place at home. Matata, our helper, told Mom that someone wanted to talk to her in the yard. As we left, we saw a van with armed soldiers. One of the soldiers wanted Mapengu to go with them. He was completely scared. Mom asked the head of the bodyguards assigned to Dad's security to reason with them and have them leave. She then called Mapengu to bring him into the living room with my aunts and cousins.

Maurice, from Belgium, was still trying to find a solution to evacuate us. But with the assassination of ten Belgian U.N. peacekeepers, the situation was tense, and priority was given to evacuating Belgian nationals living in Rwanda. Eventually, Commander Gijsbrechts obtained an agreement for us to be evacuated on one of the last flights leaving Kigali. So, we had to be ready to leave at any time.

Maurice also contacted General Huchon in Paris, the head of the France's forces abroad, who also gave him his agreement in principle. Measures would be put in place to get us out. Furthermore, he promised Maurice that we would be evacuated to France via Burundi and the Central African Republic.

As incoming international calls had become inaccessible in the evening, Maurice attempted to reach us without success. There was no instant messaging yet. As he felt relieved to have finally found a solution, he promised himself to inform us first thing the next morning, on April 12. Unfortunately, he never had the opportunity to tell us that there was a possibility of exfiltrating us from Rwanda to take us to a safe place while waiting for calm to return.

2. Exodus

Burundi

April 12

That morning I woke up with a lump in my stomach. A feeling of irrational fear overtook me. I thought it was too quiet. The kind of calm that precedes a storm.

I went to Dad's office, looking for his briefcase. Inside was the business card of Lieutenant-Colonel Jean-Jacques Maurin, his French adviser. I had seen him once or twice at home, particularly a month earlier, when Dad had received the Legion of Honor medal. So, I called him and introduced myself: "Mr. Maurin, it's Alice, Major General Nsabimana's daughter. We are still in Kiyovu, and I would like to know what is happening because we are not informed of anything and ...." Before I even had time to finish my sentence, he answered me by shouting on the phone: "What are you doing here still? It's dangerous. Most of the other families have already been evacuated. Be ready in ten minutes, I'll send you a convoy, and we'll exfiltrate you."

We will never thank him enough because it is thanks to him that we had our lives saved.

As the eldest of the family there, I felt a great responsibility towards Mom and my little brothers and sisters. Overcome by a force and a determination I did not suspect existed, everything was clear in my mind. I ran to tell

Mom the news and asked my brothers and sisters to prepare quickly. Then I grabbed the box where Mom kept all her jewelry and our passports. I also had the reflex to take Dad's briefcase. It contained some official documents, his 1994 diary, letters, photos of him recently taken at headquarters, his notebook, and his official passport.

Fortunately, each of us was efficient and prompt in getting ready for departure. What's more, all the important documents were centralized in Mom's jewelry box, which made the process easier. However, no one thought to bring a change of clothes.

It seemed to me that the convoy arrived sooner than announced. Fabrice asked if we could leave with Dumu, who had also arrived home with his family, but our Aunt Julienne told him that Dumu had to stay with his family. Immediately, we were placed in an armored vehicle. Our evacuation from Kiyovu was fast. We barely had time to wave goodbye to the extended family. Our aunts and cousins watched us depart with deep sadness. Even if we had the feeling of abandoning them, we sincerely hoped to see them again very soon ... for the funeral.

The journey was short. We arrived at the French school, located a few minutes from the house. On site, there were many expatriate families and senior Rwandan dignitaries. Seeing people with their suitcases, some with their dogs, I began to understand that we would be evacuated to a foreign country. That would not be a problem for us since we had our passports.

On the other hand, the other people seemed better prepared than we were. They had probably had more time to gather and take away the objects that were dear to them. We waited quietly and calmly. We felt people were scared and eager to leave. After a few minutes, a French soldier took the floor to say that they would call people to get into the vans. He immediately warned us that there would not be enough places for all Rwandans. So the expatriates, their families, and their pets got into the vans first. Then it was the turn for Rwandans, and we heard ourselves repeating that only one member per family could leave until the empty places were filled. I found this so unfair as I did not understand how one could prioritize evacuating pets over people. But when I think about it, it did not change anything since they traveled on their masters' laps.

They called a few names before I heard mine, "Alice Nsabimana." I did not hesitate and made my decision quickly. It was either the whole family or no one. How could I have abandoned my mother, Yvonne, Josiane, and Fabrice? Someone else took a chance. The vans filled up and drove off shortly after.

Looking back, this episode reminds me of the movie *Hotel Rwanda*, which I saw when it came out in 2004. I had not cried for several years. I found it difficult to watch the same sorting scenes because I felt as though I was reliving them. That day, I cried a lot at the end of the screening because it confronted me with a story I had personally experienced ten years earlier.

We were fortunately not left to our own devices because we were among the "personalities at risk" slated to be evacuated.[1] With people left behind, French soldiers and their armored vehicles remained to protect us. Regrettably, we could no longer take the cargo plane specially chartered for the evacuation. Another solution however soon became

---

1. List of "178 people (...) candidates for evacuation abroad on April 12, 1994." http://rwanDadelaguerreaugenocide.univ-paris1.fr/wp-content/uploads/2010/01/Annex_83.pdf

available; they told us they would escort us to Kanombe airport. No doubt, to calm us down, they also said they would try to find another cargo plane to transport us to France.

Once again, we had to take detours to get to Kanombe. The French soldiers asked us to close our eyes, but some of us did not follow their instructions. The sight was unbearable. The streets, once bustling, were strewn with corpses. They are unfortunately the last images I have of Kigali, the city that I loved so much. I still can't get rid of them.

We spent a few hours in the airport hall and were called to board a cargo plane at night. We were mainly with officials or families of wealthy Rwandans. Among us were *Hutu* dignitaries from the old regime, families of Ministers, *Tutsis*, southerners, northerners, opponents of the regime ... We were told that our final destination would be Paris, transiting through Bujumbura (the capital of neighboring Burundi), then Bangui (capital of the Central African Republic). Although the trip's outcome was uncertain, we were relieved to come out of that inferno.

Yvonne recalls being gripped by an unimaginable fear and a bad feeling when we arrived in Bujumbura. We were escorted to the airport VIP lounge by soldiers resembling those of the RPF, whom we often encountered when we passed in front of the CND (the Rwandan National Assembly). She thought we were going to die that day!

However, we felt some semblance of security for the first time in hours. We were able to drink and eat something. Then, thinking it was finally time to board, we joined other people (some of whom must have arrived in the meantime) in the airport lobby. We stayed there for endless hours without any explanation. Finally, in the evening, we saw people from the Red Cross arrive with small yellow basins, gray blankets, and soap. There were no offers of accommodation or any other explanation, so we understood that we would spend the night on the ground, in the hall of Bujumbura airport. Later, we were treated to some food. No matter. No one really felt like eating.

In the end, we remained cloistered for three days in the airport hall. The days passed slowly. We woke up and tried to find a water source to do a quick wash with the sponge we had been given. We only had the clothes we were wearing because, leaving Kigali, we expected to reach our final destination a few hours later. During the day, groups would form by generation. For my part, I was happy to have found my friend Angélique. I remember her older sister Winny was almost at the end of her pregnancy. We observed the comings and goings of the planes and discussed everything and nothing. Everybody returned to their place a few meters away in the evening. Dinner was meager: rice in bowls along with a few cans of food that no one could eat. When night fell, we slept on the floor on straw mats. This is the moment that I liked the least because we saw these same soldiers circulating among us with their weapons. Sleep was impossible with the shadows, the sound of their footsteps, and the mosquitoes that bit us as soon as the lights went out.

We still had no news of the family members who remained in Kigali or from Brussels. Maurice knew that we would be evacuated to France. Still, he had not had time to tell us since the international lines had been cut on the evening of April 11. They all must have been worried, but we could not reach them to tell them that we were stuck in Bujumbura.

April 15

In the morning, the Salvatore family, Burundian diplomat friends with whom we had lived in Tripoli (Libya) in the early '80s, came to see us at the airport. Even if their ethnicity is of no importance, given the context, I would like to specify that they were *Tutsis*. They had heard the list of people at Bujumbura airport on RPF's radio *Muhabura*. Apparently, an informant among us had managed to provide the list of people present at the airport. In fact, I recall this man who circulated in the room, noting the names of everyone present under the pretext of finding us an evacuation route. In short, our old friends brought us food and asked us if we needed anything. Mom then gave them my aunt Agnès' phone number in Brussels, asking them to let them know that we had been stuck in Bujumbura for a few days and asked if they could find a way to get us out of there. Naturally, we would be eternally grateful to them.

Zaire

On April 16, the Burundian airport authorities informed us that we would have to vacate the premises in preparation for the planned national funeral of President Ntaryamira, whose body and those of his companions would soon be returned to their homeland. Meanwhile, our flight to Paris was not yet possible. So we were given the option to leave the airport and be temporarily housed in hangars near the airport or evacuate to Bukavu, the capital of the province of South Kivu in Zaire, now the Democratic Republic of the Congo.

The adults present did not have to think long and opted for Zaire. Most of us, even the youngest, remembered Burundi's unrest in 1988, marked by the Ntega and Marangara inter-ethnic massacres. Although I was only eleven years old then, I will never forget the sight of bodies, including those of children tied to straw mats, streaming into Lake Rweru while on summer vacation in Bugesera. In addition to this cruelty, still very present in our minds, the fact that President Ndadaye had been assassinated six months earlier led us to a very clear choice. The adults were talking simultaneously, saying they would not risk going to the middle of nowhere for fear of being forgotten. Our parents, Hutus and Tutsis, were united in their decisions. Even though our country was sinking into flames, there was no need to tempt fate and risk our lives. They, therefore, unanimously chose Bukavu.

During the afternoon, we gathered the very few things we had to board a cargo plane to Zaire. In their kindness, the Salvatore family returned to see us with a few spare clothes before we left Bujumbura.

After nights on the floor, eating tasteless food, and fearing for our lives, this little journey almost sounded like a trip to a heavenly place, so oppressive was our environment. When we arrived in Bukavu, we were picked up by Zairian soldiers who made us cross the town and go into a sort of auditorium. It felt good to see normal streets without corpses and with music playing, and to see the red dust rising as we drove. It reminded us of the roads of Kigali before the onslaught of violence. We immediately felt on familiar and secure ground. An official took the floor to welcome us, followed by another, smaller man but who had a certain charisma. The latter, Mr. Jacques Kyembwa, was the governor of South Kivu. He spoke distinctly, in perfect French, and he commanded respect. He welcomed us to Zaire and added that we must be tired and hungry and that he would not hold us any longer, but that we would see him again very soon. In a few minutes, he managed to gain our trust by responding to our most urgent needs: hunger and security. Then, with a discreet nod, he gave his orders. Five minutes later, we found ourselves in the same vehicles that had brought us back from the airport. We were not sure exactly where we were going. But that did not matter. We were far from Rwanda and Burundi and knew we could trust Governor Kyembwa's word.

The vehicles took us to the Riviera Hotel in Bukavu, where we spent a few days housed and fed. We felt like homeless people who suddenly found themselves in a five-star hotel. There was even a swimming pool. We slept again in beds with sheets, ate three meals a day, and even drank Fanta. We regained a little taste for life and the few pounds lost since that fateful night of April 6.

The days passed quietly. Our parents spared us the news, filtering out the horrors that continued to unfold in Rwanda. Instead, they were busy looking for a solution for us to reach different destinations in Europe. Most of us were still children and teenagers. We spent our time playing in the hotel courtyard and the swimming pool. Josiane almost drowned there one day, trying to swim in the adult pool. She was fortunately caught in extremis by Landry, who brought her back to the edge. We did not know if and when we could return to Kigali. In addition, we still expected that the situation would return to normal so we would be able to organize the funeral.

From Bukavu, we were able to get in touch with the members of our family who remained in Kigali. In late April, we learned we could cross the border to see our maternal uncle Athanase in Cyangugu, the province bordering on Bukavu in western Rwanda. Returning to Rwanda terrified us as if we were going to throw ourselves into harm's way.

Our former bodyguards dressed in plain clothes escorted us in an anonymous "combi" van driven by Baudoin, who came specially to pick us up. The crossing went without a hitch. We passed a few roadblocks manned by the Rwandan Armed Forces. Castar's name was still popular and acted as a pass if there was any doubt about our identities.

We had arranged to meet at a hotel in Cyangugu. Our uncle Athanase was already waiting for us. It did us the greatest good to see a familiar face again and hear Kinyarwanda, our mother tongue. Indeed, we were beginning to get used to hearing Swahili and even learning a few words.

Mom could withdraw funds from their account thanks to our uncle Athanase who worked at the National Bank of Rwanda. She slipped this subsistence money he brought in her bra, as women did. He had also brought back two whole suitcases with our personal belongings, including clothes, shoes, accessories, and bags. There was even my diary in which my last entry was dated April 6, 1994. That diary entry mentioned that I had to complete my letter to Denise and Maurice with the list of everything Dad and Mom were to bring me from Belgium the following week.

Our uncle gave us news of the family. Most had left the Kiyovu residence after our hasty departure. Some had returned to their homes, while others had insisted on staying with our grandmother in Dad's native village in Ruhengeri. Everyone was very worried. Despite believing that we had already arrived in Belgium, the family had heard a few days earlier that the RPF Radio Muhabura had reported our presence at the airport of Bujumbura. Some even thought we were dead. The rest of the news was not good. Although I was only half listening, I heard that the killings were intensifying, the city was ablaze, and a transitional government had been appointed. In a hurry to unpack the things he had brought back and for fear of falling back into that trauma, I had to turn a deaf ear to the news. Finally, I had heard enough and walked out into the hotel lobby. We had a meal together in the restaurant.

We said goodbye at the end of the afternoon to return to Bukavu before nightfall. We hoped to see our uncle Athanase again soon in Rwanda.

I did not know yet that I would face the greatest fear of my life and only fear God from that day on. My co-workers, who wonder why they've never seen me stressed out to the point of losing control, will find the explanation for my legendary calm in the following.

I was so excited about arriving at the Riviera Hotel and finishing unpacking all the belongings that I paid no attention to what was happening on the road. Instead, I wondered if someone had thought of packing my favorite dresses and necklaces. Or had they thought of slipping several pairs of shoes into the suitcase? Lost in my thoughts, I did not even notice that we stopped at a roadblock just a few minutes after getting on the road. Surprised, I then looked up.

Two men walked up to our van. They were Interahamwe militiamen. I knew they were militiamen because I had already seen them on television in news reports about their political party's rallies. They had no firearms, only machetes. To the rear, on the right, there were a few people, men, and women, whose expressions of terror and anguish I will never forget. It's as if they knew their time had already come.

One of the militiamen advanced on the driver's side, another on the passenger side where a bodyguard dressed in civilian clothes was seated. We were all spread out in the back. Mom, Josiane, and Fabrice were in the middle while Yvonne, me, and another bodyguard were in the back. They inspected the vehicle and the passengers with bloodshot eyes and asked where we were going. Baudoin replied that we were the family of the late Castar and that they were going to shelter us in Bukavu. The two men did not seem happy with his answer and asked for our ID cards. During this time, two other militiamen, who had just appeared, walked around the combi to scrutinize us closely. One of them, who looked full of hatred and anger and had a sweaty brow and whom I will never forget, stopped at my level, pointed his machete at my head, looked me straight in the eye, and shouted: "*Wowe, sohoka*," which meant, "You, get out of the car." My heart felt like it jumped out of my chest, and I thought I would pee myself. I could not think anymore. I was so scared. I heard Mom exclaim, "No, she will not get out of the car!"

The bodyguard seated in the back, next to Yvonne, said to him: "This is the daughter of Major General Déogratias Nsabimana, Castar, who has just perished in the presidential plane." The militiaman retorted: "Castar never had a *Tutsi* child."

At this precise moment, I had the reflex to inflate my nostrils (historically, since the institution of ethnic groups, the *Hutus* were reputed to be recognizable by their large noses). I also remembered that I had my card for officers' dependents in my belongings, with my picture alongside Dad's. My photo also showed nostrils of a decent size. Because at this precise moment, it was only that which could, unfortunately, save me! We were in full ethnic profiling mode!

There was parleying for a time that seemed like an eternity; our ID cards circulated in front, including mine for military children. A few bank notes were also exchanged (probably some that had been saved inside Dad's jacket, which a soldier from the presidential guard had returned to Mom, or perhaps some of the subsistence money brought by Uncle Athanase). Then, finally, things calmed down after endless minutes. They ended up ordering us to leave. No other order had ever sounded so sweet to my ears.

The car sped off with a bang, and we left there, all traumatized. I was like a zombie, eyes closed for the rest of the trip, thinking especially of those poor people who begged us with their eyes and whose fate I sadly imagined. I had just escaped death. God had probably decided that my time had not yet come. All the way back to Bukavu, I cried silently.

In Kinyarwanda, we say: *Imana yirirwa ahandi igataha i Rwanda*, which means God spends his day elsewhere and returns to Rwanda. But what had happened to our "land of a thousand hills?" Why did God not want to come home anymore? How could the Devil have taken possession of the hearts of men to the point of savagely killing their fellow citizens? From that day on, I was never again scared to the point of losing my wits. From that day, I put a mental block on Rwanda because this was the last image that remained with me before crossing the border. For years, I refused to listen to anything about Rwanda, which I considered cursed, whether on the radio or elsewhere. Even the sound of my mother tongue, Kinyarwanda, was no longer melodious to my ears.

I had always heard that hypocrisy was one of our character traits. But how could one lose sight of one's neighbor's humanity? This was a dimension that completely escaped me. All this for what, when I had grown up knowing that *Hutus* and *Tutsis* spoke the same language and shared the same culture to the point of marrying each other! I no longer wanted anything to do with "those people," even if they were my compatriots.

For that reason, I promised myself not to marry a Rwandan. (Those who have made good-hearted attempts to settle me with compatriots find the answer here.) It took me a while to relearn and appreciate what Rwandan culture can offer. And it is an understatement to say all the riches it possesses!

The return to the Riviera Hotel ended well. Once we had crossed the border, there was nothing more to fear anyway. It was even a blessing that we were surrounded by Zairians. During the days that followed, I was quiet. I dwelt on the scene we had experienced. I kept thinking that I could have died that day if the militiamen had insisted on getting me out of the vehicle. I managed to free up my mind by reading a novel by Danielle Steel, an author whose books I started devouring the previous year after reading *Jewels*.

Mom informed us a few days later that there was a possibility of leaving imminently for Paris. However, the governor of Bukavu had offered to accommodate my sister Yvonne and me at his home for the remainder of the school year at the Belgian school. For my little sister, Josiane, and my little brother, Fabrice, who were eleven and nine years old respectively, the early end of the school year was less serious. It was a difficult choice we obviously did not want to make because we did not want to be separated. Yet, the decision was made in our best interests. We barely had time to settle down when things turned upside down again.

That same evening, we were all invited to eat with the Kyembwa family. We arrived at their huge villa, where we were welcomed by Governor Kyembwa, his wife, *Maman* Catherine, and their two children, little Jean-Jacques, nicknamed "Gigi," and Yvette, who was a year younger than I. The first contact was formal and intimidating. We had not chosen to be there, and even though we felt immediately welcome, we felt somewhat bitter. The parents were warm, while the children seemed to wonder what we were doing there. The first dinner was memorable: I had never found myself in a situation where there was a butler, dressed in white, holding a basin for each of us to wash our hands, and who then remained there for the meal. I thought I was in *Gone with the Wind*.

The meal was delicious. Mom, who still had to prepare the luggage, said goodbye, promising to come back to pick us up soon. She also asked us to be exemplary in our behavior towards our benefactors. There was no question of us embarrassing her!

After our mother and the little ones had left, *Maman* Catherine took us upstairs to a room Yvonne and I would share. She showed us our beds, wardrobes, and private bathroom and then said a prayer with us. Before leaving, she hugged us to wish us good night. She was very kind throughout our stay with them, which offered great emotional relief. We cannot thank her enough for being a mother during this difficult time.

The first nights in Bukavu were complicated. Yvonne cried a lot. It was the first time that our family nucleus was dissolved. She kept listening to the news on the radio in our room, which did not help matters as the situation in Rwanda, on the other side of Lake Kivu, continued to deteriorate. We had no news from Denise and Maurice. Besides, Dad's body was still lying somewhere in a cold room. We kept thinking about his funeral.

Mom then flew to Kinshasa with Josiane, Fabrice, and Didier, our cousin, who joined them in Bukavu just before their departure. He also brought back some of Dad's precious documents. They were welcomed by the Rwandan ambassador to Zaire, Etienne Sengegera, who put them up while waiting for a French visa.

The change in climate was impressive, according to them. While Bukavu was tropical, Kinshasa was hot and humid. Shortly after their arrival, Josiane got very ill, almost on the verge of death. Mom was scared, fearing another misfortune would strike us when we had not even started mourning for Dad yet. Josiane remembers that she could barely walk but keeps the memory of Mom, strong and positive intact. She did not see her lose hope once. Josiane spent her time in bed. She ate almost nothing but constantly had to go to the bathroom, either carried by our Mom or crawling if there was no one to help her. Frustratingly, she heard the children playing outside but couldn't go out and join them.

For Yvonne and me, the situation improved as time went by. Gigi and Yvette very quickly considered us "invited guests" rather than "visitors." We still laugh about it.

The first positive culture shock occurred when we arrived at Bukavu's Belgian school. The Zairians' warmth and outspokenness, by nature more extroverted than the Rwandans, was our first remedy to avoid sinking into depression. I found them naturally more modern in their way of speaking, thinking, and even dressing. What is funny and what my longtime friend Jean-Louis confided to me is that he and his friends thought that we Rwandans had "raised the standard." He was impressed by the fact that I changed my clothes daily, especially my Michael Jackson jacket, which was very trendy then and very few people wore it at the Belgian school in Bukavu. He still remembers the day when, having taken off my braids, I arrived with my hair down and the boys wondered if it was mine. Obviously, I was unaware of that, and above all, I thought I was too "backwards" compared to the other girls. Go figure!

I was in a great class, and I was able to quickly make Zairian friends. We found some compatriots in our situation, who had arrived from Rwanda. Some of them had come the same way as us since fleeing Kanombe airport.

I also met Rwandans living in Bukavu for several years, some of whom had never known Rwanda and did not speak Kinyarwanda. It was not the time to talk politics. It was still too early. They did not dare ask me the details of our escape, and I did not dare ask how they came to live in Bukavu.

Given the situation, it was weird to think that there were carefree young people who laughed and organized dance parties right next to Rwanda, like we used to be at the Belgian school in Kigali. Nonetheless, we lived a few months of relative normalcy. It was a breath of fresh air that, for one term, allowed me to take a break from my mourning and gain momentum for the rest of the adventure.

We went "home" for lunch almost every noon. It was simpler and no valet was holding a basin for us. *Maitre*, the cook, regaled us with his good cuisine. We liked the pasta and lasagna day. It must have been Wednesdays, if I remember correctly. *Papa* Kyembwa loved *fufu* (a dough made with cassava flour), served daily. *Maman* Catherine continued to shower us with her sweet benevolence.

From time to time, we heard from Mom through the Governor, but we heard very little about Rwanda, or else they spared the details for us.

One day, the Kyembwa's watchman came to tell us that a gentleman from our family had come to visit us and wanted to take us to Cyangugu to see the other family members.

Papa Kyembwa came down, telling us to stay there. I remember that scene. Our tutor asked me if I recognized him, and I said yes, it was Uncle Athanase, Mom's brother. Although the Governor authorized us to greet our uncle, he categorically refused to let us leave. He explained to him politely but firmly, with all his authority, "their mother entrusted me with her children, for whom I am responsible. She did not allow me to let them go out with anyone, so I'm sorry, they do not move from here." Our maternal uncle, a parent, surely understood this precautionary measure. As a parent, I would certainly do the same.

Yvonne gradually regained a taste for life. She met some friends with whom she went swimming in Lake Kivu. It was the era of the *Beverly Hills* series and of teenagers her age comparing their outfits and inventing choreographies on rap or R&B music. Yvonne has always been a gifted dancer; she even invented a dance step that left her comrades in awe.

As for my generation, as some had already reached the age of majority and could drive, we sometimes met at Yvette's to swim in the lake (this was easy there because their residence was right by the lake), and sometimes at other friends' places. Yvette would then drive her little car, or Bismos would come and pick us up, accompanied by Andy, Ghislain, or Tif.

France

The rest of the family who had gone to Kinshasa had to delay their departure so Mom could obtain visas for France. Around mid-May, they finally flew to Paris. When they arrived on French soil, they were surprised by the cold, even though it must have been around 20 degrees Celsius (or 68 Fahrenheit). It was very different from the heat of Kinshasa.

Mom took a family room at the Ibis hotel. With Maurice's help from a distance, she devoted her time to administrative procedures to reach Belgium, where we had more family ties. Didier's presence was a great support. He assisted her as best he could, taking care of the little ones when Mom had to run errands. Didier sadly passed away a few years later. He was unable to overcome the trauma of the war.

For Fabrice, it was rather pleasant to stay at the hotel. He especially enjoyed the hearty breakfast. Josiane, who was still weak when she arrived, was able to receive treatment. Once back on her feet, she spent her time listening to music. Billy Ze Kick's song "Mangez Moi" (French: "Eat Me") was playing on the radio.

Money melted away faster than snow in the sun. The small sum that Mom had was almost used up, more than half having been used to pay the militiamen to let us go. There had been no other way to get more funds.

A week later, with no other help and no longer able to afford the Ibis, Mom had no choice but to board everyone in a modest hotel in the 13th arrondissement. It was a single room worthy of the "slum landlords" with dark beige walls that did not appear to have ever been painted and a tiny window that did not allow light in. There was not even a bathroom, just a small sink in the room that they used to wash with a washcloth. Mom shared the bed with Josiane and Fabrice while Didier slept on the hide-a-bed whose mattress had lost half its foam. This episode rather amused Fabrice because he felt secure being so close together. He could also watch cartoons and the adventure show *Fort Boyard*. What more could a nine-year-old want?

Food was also scarce. For breakfast, which had to be eaten as late as possible to try to combine it with lunch, Mom would buy two *mitraillettes* (sandwiches made from

French bread with meat, salad, and fries) that she let them eat as much as they wanted along with a little water and fruit juice. Unfortunately, she had lost her appetite as she was too busy thinking about their means of survival. Didier tried his best to get Josiane to eat. He sang at the top of his lungs, and since he did not speak Kinyarwanda well, the younger ones constantly made fun of him.

Maurice arrived as the messiah a few days later. They were all relieved to see him arrive, laughing and crying with relief. Maurice landed in this chaotic environment, laden with food like Rambo. They packed up and left the hotel a few days later.

Maurice had sacrificed part of his scholarship to help Mom financially.

Belgium

Maurice, Mom, Didier, Josiane, and Fabrice were welcomed with open arms by our maternal aunt Agnès and her husband, Augustin, in their two-bedroom apartment. Though the space was small, it was good to be together as a family in a warm environment.

Denise, who had resumed classes at the the Brussels Management School, ICHEC, was trying to live through her mourning as best she could. In a short period, she had gone from a Rwandan student, scholarship holder, and daughter of General Nsabimana to being exiled. She felt like she was living a bad dream. Around her, everything ran as usual while her world collapsed. During the day, she felt like an automaton, getting up, dressing mechanically, and then attending lectures. Sometimes the tears flowed by themselves while she was riding the subway or sitting in class. Life had taken another turn. What was most insane in the story is that the attack on the presidential plane completely changed our lives, plunging us into immense sadness and uncertainty. For other Rwandans in the diaspora, however, that terrorist act was synonymous with joy. It meant that they would finally be able to return freely to Rwanda. Denise remembers that day when she had met a group of Rwandans, among whom was Lina, a *Tutsi* friend. She broke away from the group, approaching Denise to say affectionately, "My condolences, dear friend. I learned that your Dad was on the plane." Denise was extremely touched by this gesture and hopes she will one day have the opportunity to see Lina again to thank her.

In Bukavu, June 1994, as was the case at the end of March of the same year in Kigali before the school holidays, ended with a few parties. Yvonne and I made it through the school year, sadly knowing our Zairian adventure would soon end.

Mom and Maurice came to get us at the end of the month. Our reunion was moving. We barely had time to bid farewell to our host family and my sister "Kelly," alias Yvette, when we found ourselves in a jeep headed for the Cyangugu army base. A helicopter piloted by Captain Aaron, whom we had previously known in Kigali, was waiting for us. We flew to Goma via Gisenyi. Very quickly, we were plunged back into a climate of terror. I had hoped that I would not have to cross the border back into Rwanda or pass a roadblock with militiamen or be trapped by the RPF. The one-hour flight was fraught with danger. At one point, the pilot had to fly very low to "avoid shots." I remember that we almost slammed into electrical wires.

Finally, we arrived in Goma. And that was the start of a long journey. Our flight to Brussels transited through Kinshasa, the capital of then Zaire (now the Democratic Republic of the Congo).

After more than fifteen hours of travel, we arrived at the Zaventem airport in Brussels. Our journey continued for a few hours. Mom and Maurice underwent a long interrogation at the border post. It was partly linked to our passports that the Belgian customs suspected were not in order. Maurice and Mom spent hours explaining who we were and how far we had come. I remember that at one point, a policeman asked me if this was really my mother because she looked very young (or I looked older). Finally, after a few hours and the validation of our passports by the customs authorities, we were able to leave the airport, ready to start a new life in Belgium. We were both excited and relieved to reach our final destination.

3. Transition

At the end of June, we met Denise, Didier, Josiane, and Fabrice at our aunt and uncle's apartment. We were so happy that the siblings were finally reunited. For our first evening, an excellent meal awaited us, Aunt Agnès' legendary *gratin dauphinois*, served with chicken thighs and steamed green beans. Our meal conversations covered several topics and we carefully avoided Rwanda at first. We were happy to discover how much our cousins Rémi and Sabrina had grown. We had seen them during the summer before in 1993 when they visited Kigali. Fabrice and Josiane went to play in the bedroom after the meal. At the same time, we settled in the living room after clearing away, washing the dishes, and cleaning the kitchen.

The evening was very emotional. For long hours, we shared various stories from the evening of April 6, 1994, until our flight. All were mesmerized, in a bewildered and attentive silence, unable to hold back their tears as we described the horror we had experienced.

Finally it was bedtime. There were two bedrooms in the apartment. Suffice it to say that we were in tight quarters. In Rwanda, we sometimes watched African films caricaturing trundle beds. It amused us to see fifteen people living together in a small house. We were not far off the mark with eleven of us for two rooms. The first night, Rémi and Sabrina slept with their parents while Mom, Josiane, and Yvonne shared the children's room. Maurice, Didier, and Fabrice slept in the living room while Denise shared her student accommodation with me. This arrangement lasted several weeks because we had nowhere to go nor enough money to rent accommodations suitable for our group.

The excitement of the first days passed as we told each other about our experiences. But then we had to quickly move on to serious things such as finding accommodation, a school, and, most importantly, papers to remain in Belgium.

For Mom, these first months were therefore very difficult. She was scared but had to keep going regardless. Finding herself suddenly widowed at forty-three with seven dependent children is not how she had imagined her future just a few months earlier. In one fell swoop she lost her husband and everything they had built during their twenty-five years of living together. During our last family getaway to Akagera National Park,[2] Mom and Dad had said that on their twenty-fifth wedding anniversary, they would renew their vows and throw a beautiful reception. That was one of the rare occasions when I saw my parents exchange

---

2. Akagera National Park is a park extending over 1122 km^2 in the northeast of Rwanda. It was created to preserve the animals of the savannah, mountains, and marshes.

tender gestures. In Rwandan and other African cultures, public displays of affection are not so common in romantic relationships, as they are deemed to be private matters. In any case, that is how things were in those years.

For Mom, all that mattered, and she always praised God for that, was that all her children were alive. Her priority was to feed us and make us study, in short, make us grow. She did not know where to start. When we were in Rwanda, the roles were fairly well shared. Mom took care of the interior and the discipline, and Dad assisted her. Now she was going to have to take on everything, right down to parent meetings, a task that used to be done by Dad. She had to be, in a way, both our father and mother, a role she carried out marvelously, like a chef!

With the support of her sister Agnès and her husband, Mom could organize herself. Maurice, who was supposed to return to Austria, decided to stay in Belgium to help her with this task.

The RPF took power at the beginning of July, so our family could no longer foresee returning to Rwanda safely. Mom with Denise and Maurice, the only adults, then spent the following weeks lining up at the Belgian Immigration Office to apply for political asylum. Since I was still a minor for a few months, I could not accompany them there. It was a scary time. I remember that the first decision we received was an "Order to leave the Belgian territory within 48 days for an unfounded request." How could these decision-makers minimize our need for a host country so brazenly? Dad had just died in an attack, and many Rwandans perished. At the same time, the country was set ablaze in unprecedented massacres, and our fate would undeniably be the same if we ventured to set foot in Rwanda again! However, my uncle Augustin reassured us that this was an obligatory step and that we had to fight and continue the procedure.

After several refusals and hours of interviews at the Office of the Commissioner General for Refugees and Stateless Persons (CGRS), we finally obtained the golden ticket: a Provisional Residence Permit authorizing us to stay in Belgium for a few months. This was already a first victory.

In August, Mom obtained social housing in Jette. It was a three-bedroom apartment, and we had more space. She registered us at the Athénée Royal and the Aurore elementary schools in Jette. Her biggest concern was providing us with an education so we could later find work and fend for ourselves.

Mom was forced to adapt to the new circumstances. Professionally, while she had been a trader in Rwanda, she could not pursue the same occupation in Belgium, at least in the first years with all of us. She, therefore, chose to train as a nurse's aide, which helped her find odd jobs, including cleaning and caring for the elderly. It paid for food and education, which was the main thing. As children and teenagers, we did not grasp the extent of her efforts. She, who had house staff a few months earlier, now did some of the same tasks for others without ever complaining. I tip my hat to her and thank her again for this rigorous and simple education she persistently instilled in us. Otherwise, we would have been powerless in the face of this brutal change in our way of life.

With so many dependent children to clothe and feed, making ends meet was not always easy. So, we had to find some tricks. Fricadelles and fries from the Aldi supermarket chain came in handy at the end of the month. Sometimes we went to get food from the Jette Social Aid service, which collected unsold supermarket items. To dress, we turned to the Petits Riens second-hand shops. Already, Josiane revealed her talents as a fashion designer. She artfully combined clothes and enhanced them with little accessories to give them a new life, sometimes more elegant than the original.

I quickly realized that if I wanted to dress like the other teenage girls I knew or buy hair products, I had to find a way to earn my own money. So I developed my talents as a hairdresser. I knew how to do braids like no one else. In Rwanda, my sister Denise had been my first guinea pig. So I "professionalized" my skills and taught my sisters Yvonne and Josiane how to braid hair. Josiane, too young, contented herself at the beginning with learning how to "finish the ends" on her dolls, that is to say, finish the braid in length. At the same time, Yvonne and I began to braid at the root. We were a pretty good trio. Occasionally, Denise joined us to help us. Very quickly, we built up a small client base. It was convenient for Mom because she could save hairdresser costs simultaneously and for us because we earned our pocket money.

Once the logistical emergencies were handled, Mom and the other widows plunged into the legal aspect. Maurice and other children of the victims assisted our mothers in initiating a legal proceeding or arbitration to obtain compensation from Rwanda's National Insurance Company (Sonarwa) for their husbands' deaths. Mom legitimately hoped that this money would allow us later to finance our university education and be the basis for the acquisition of decent housing for our family. But we were never compensated. In short, the procedure that began at the end of May 1994 with the declaration of the loss of the Falcon Mystere 50 aircraft registered 9XR-NN by the cabinet of the Presidency of Rwanda with the insurer Sonarwa ended in failure in 1998. The Court of First Instance of Kigali requested the seizure of the funds supposed to compensate the survivors of the attack victims. We learned later that these funds, which were rightfully ours, were diverted to Kigali, despite a court order that had been issued to transfer them to the families of the victims of the attack of April 6, 1994.

Despite these setbacks, Mom did not give up. She had to manage things differently, juggling several jobs and the little extras we brought back thanks to the braids. The biggest lesson learned from these years, and that Mom keeps telling her grandchildren and us, is to be persistent, patient, and positive in everything we do. She says that the car accident Dad had a year before his death paradoxically prepared her to assume responsibilities on her own, which she did remarkably well.

Rwanda remained sadly famous, and we continued to follow with horror the news of what was happening in our country. The number of deaths continued to increase. News reports showed massacres and bodies strewn in the streets. The scale of the killings was such that the word "genocide" had replaced the word "war." Moreover, the massive displacement of refugees to neighboring countries and the images of cholera and dysentery in the makeshift camps foreshadowed a curse for our people.

We had to face the facts: a return to Rwanda was becoming increasingly unlikely. It's hard to imagine that I was a carefree teenager a few months ago, with my revolts, dreams, and fears. I had already mapped out my life over the next few years. At the end of secondary school, I would come to study in Belgium, like Denise. I did not know yet which course of study to take since Dad had discouraged me from pursuing my path in the hotel business. Since I was naturally independent, I thought that I would not return to Rwanda for each holiday but would visit European countries. After my education, I had told myself I would return to Rwanda permanently, find a job and settle down in my own home. Like my cousins, I never dreamed of getting married early. I thought twenty-eight was a perfect age. Dad liked to say that since he would be retired, he would multiply the cows for his daughters' dowries.[3] I imagined him accompanying me to the altar. Then a sumptuous reception would be held in our residence in Ndera or Nyakinama, as parties were sometimes organized there, and the venue was suitable. Obviously, my husband would be a Rwandan, tall and dark like Dad. He would certainly be from a "good family."

But alas, all my teenage concerns seemed to go up in smoke. Along with my shattered dreams, something snapped inside me, shattering my trust in my people. I was greatly disappointed by my compatriots when I saw the butchery in which the Rwandan people had indulged since 1990, and certainly even before. Yet the reference for me was that period during which I could understand what was happening around me. I could not imagine that human beings could commit such atrocities towards their brothers and sisters. No human being should die under such conditions.

Considering myself lucky to have survived with my mother, brothers, and sisters, I even concealed the fact that I was a victim. The shooting down of the presidential

---

3. In Rwanda, the dowry is of great importance. The future husband must bring goods as gifts to the girl's family. Generally, cows were offered, the number and quality depending on the status of the families.

plane with Dad inside, in which two sitting presidents and officials had nevertheless perished, was treated like a non-event. It was as if the plane had fallen on its own, which implied that we had to walk with our heads down or keep a low profile when we talked about Rwandan victims. It was as if we could not mourn our loved ones.

Denise had the same feeling: her lifeline was broken. Before the fateful date of April 6, she saw herself returning to Rwanda with her ICHEC college degree in hand after having taken the time to explore the world. She imagined working in a bank or a state corporation, getting married with a big ceremony in which there would be a big buffet. There would of course also be platters of fried potatoes and pieces of meat, as often seen at weddings where dishes were served outside for *abavumbyi,* or uninvited guests or freeloaders that under Rwandan custom were required to be served food and drinks. She saw herself living in a house made with bricks with all the comforts possible and having children and traveling during the holidays. In short, she was thinking of the traditional life of the Rwandan elite, all mapped out, without pitfalls. Her dreams were completely shattered when, a few weeks earlier, she had started lining up for long hours at the Immigration Office to petition for political asylum.

We passed the end of the summer quietly. I often squatted in Denise's student flat. I missed my new Zairian friends terribly. I often wrote to Yvette, who gave me regular news from Bukavu. A few friends from Rwanda were also gradually arriving along with many other Rwandans who had fled like us. Looking back, I think we did quite well in avoiding feeling sorry for ourselves. As I saw it, we had arrived without our personal belongings, without clothes, with just our dignity to move forward.

The school year started very quickly. It was hard to imagine that only five months had passed since that cursed April 6th. With the history of Rwanda being fresh in people's minds, we had the sympathy of the director of the Athénée Royal de Jette, who passed the word on to our teachers. At school, as soon as I said that I was Rwandan, the first awkward question was: "Ah, are you *Hutu* or *Tutsi*?" I always tried to answer that it did not matter because my status as a political refugee had been provoked by this pseudodifferentiation, whereas among "us" we could not even tell each other apart. I read a lot of empathy in the eyes of some and pity in the eyes of others. Overall, my school integration was successful, and I quickly had a few girlfriends who made my stay pleasant. It was nevertheless uncanny to see young people around us living normally with the worries of teenagers or the inevitable topic of dieting for young girls, while we constantly had Rwanda on our minds. What was going on there? Could we go back one day? Could we bury Dad?

It was especially difficult for Yvonne, who was in the same school as me, to see the other students so carefree when she felt like the sky had fallen on her head. She struggled to fit in, not speaking to her teachers or classmates.

For Fabrice and Josiane, who did not speak French well, the start of the new school year was relatively easy. The other children were generous and understanding. They had been warned that newcomers from Rwanda were arriving and were certainly traumatized. At first, some classmates made fun of their accents. Being impulsive and explosive, Josiane slapped one of them. That act earned her the respect of others, and from then on instead of making fun of her, they taught her the language, allowing her little by little to gain self-confidence.

Some teachers took them under their wing, giving them extra grammar and mathematics lessons. All this was just a simple jaunt for them, an adventure they lived through with innocence and lightness. After all, it was nice to run outside, play basketball and come home and play video games at friends' houses.

Within months, we began to adopt an almost normal life as young teenagers. My friends from the Belgian school in Kigali were gradually arriving in Belgium. From time to time, we went to spend the weekend in Zaventem with Gustave's family. I remember that we all slept together because several of their cousins and other friends came simultaneously. Gustave had a big family. I can still see their mother cooking several chickens and heaps of fries to feed everyone. Today, I tell myself that we were irresponsible in imposing this on parents. But at the same time, they transmitted this value of sharing to us.

We were slowly managing to become carefree again, despite the hardships we had been through. We also reconnected with Corneille, who was living in Germany. One weekend, he joined us. I think we were at Gustave's with a few other friends. We told each other about our escape from Rwanda and our paths. Corneille commanded our admiration. That evening, he told us with dignity about that cursed night in April 1994 when he lost his entire family. My blood was frozen, and I wondered how he managed to still stand. But he seemed calm and said that his new adoptive family from Germany was wonderful. We talked about our dreams. The next day, we had a picnic at the *Parc de la Jeunesse* in Jette. The afternoon ended with Corneille's mesmerizing acapella songs.

Between the end of 1994 and 1996, we began to look at the future in a positive light again. It could not be otherwise. We gratefully realized that life had given us a "second chance." What a joy to be in a place where we did not hear gunshots.

From what we observed around us, the Rwandans who found themselves refugees adapted very well, either by learning a new trade or reinventing themselves. As far as my memories go back and according to the reputation given to my compatriots, Rwandans of all stripes are proud and hardworking.

Our community therefore imported what is most beautiful. Some elders thought of perpetuating our culture by creating a traditional dance group called *Inyange*. *Inyange* means white heron, which, when it spreads its wings, reflects the image of Rwandan dancers who mainly use their arms. I can still see my mother sewing the first outfits. At the same time, Aunt Agnès, the tireless Claudia and Nancy, and the Murenzi were busy finishing our first show. And it was a success. The group has grown and continues on till today. With the development of the Rwandan community came festive events, such as weddings, baptisms, and communions. *Inyange* was often part of the party, the troupe animating the celebrations. Our shows also became like therapy for many of us, and our songs would recount the life rituals back home. Almost three decades later, I am proud to introduce my daughters to traditional Rwandan dance.

Fabrice, Josiane, Yvonne, and I were part of the dance troupe and are grateful for the guidance and discipline we received there. In addition to allowing us to exert ourselves physically, the smile permanently illuminating the faces of the dancers brought back memories of the time when Dad took us to his hometown in Ruhengeri in the north of Rwanda, where we danced the *Hinga amasaka* with village children. Rwandan dance represents a real moment of joy and sharing.

While we continued our reconstruction in Belgium, for people in our families who remained in Rwanda, bad news unfortunately kept pouring in. Among those who had been able to flee from Rwanda to Zaire, many of my cousins died of cholera in refugee camps near Goma, where Rwandans had fled by the thousands.

In 1997, after the forced evacuation of these same camps towards Rwanda, my three paternal aunts, Généreuse, Dative, and Esther, with their husbands and some of my cousins, my maternal grandparents, and several family members were brutally murdered. Some were shot, and others burned alive in their homes. Their only crime was to have been directly linked to the Nsabimana family. We learned that my aunt Esther, who looked like Dad's twin sister, was paraded like a trophy before being shot in the public square in front of her children. Dad's native Ryinyo sector was completely destroyed, leaving only a few widows and their children. Having seen all her children decimated one after the other, my paternal grandmother died of a heart attack. The executioners were cynical enough to let her witness the death of her children. The only survivor was my aunt Julienne, who died a few years later following an illness.

There have been assassinations, summary executions, and
ill-treatment of people for their simple relationship with
Major-General Déogratias Nsabimana, who lost his life
during the April 6, 1994, attack against the plane of the
Rwandan President.

Clearly, a Machiavellian extermination campaign indis-
criminately targeted most of the relatives of this former
dignitary. For example, the hunt for close relatives has
already cost the lives of the following relatives

- In December 1996, his nephew, by marriage, Mr. Fidèle
  KARANGWA, a 31-year-old shopkeeper, was kid-
  napped in Kampala when he went to see his truck. He
  was deported to Rwanda, where he was imprisoned and
  tortured to death in the special prison of Ruhengeri.

- On March 5, 1997, his brother-in-law, Mr. Léopold
  RUTEBUKA (57 years old), a communal civil servant,
  was shot dead near his home in broad morning daylight
  on his way to work at the Nyamutera communal office.

- At the current rate, the entire family of the former
  Chief of Staff of the Rwandan army is about to be exter-
  minated. Until recently, General Déogratias' mother,
  Marcianne NYIRAMBONA (85 years old), suffered
  the destruction of her home by RPA soldiers twice, in
  addition to the moral torture constantly inflicted on her
  by the killings mentioned above in which her children
  and grandchildren were taken from her one by one. In
  March 1997, her sheet-metal home was set on fire by
  RPA soldiers stationed at Mugogwe military camp who
  came in a van very early in the morning to the Ryinyo

sector. Currently, this octogenarian lives with neighbors whereas she had decent housing.

- On April 17, 1997, his uncle, Mr. NTIBANYURWA (+/-60 years old), and the latter's son KATABARWA, a 37-year-old teacher, were murdered in Ryinyo in Nkuli commune.
- On Wednesday, June 4, 1997, his brother-in-law, Mr. Célestin NGULINZIRA, a teacher, was assassinated with his three children. They are:
-

1. His son Bernard Twahirwa (25) who was an Air-Rwanda agent;
2. His daughter Alphonsine Dusabemariya (22), who was a registered nurse;
3. His son Jean de Dieu Ngulinzira (under 14), who was in 6th grade.

- On June 13, 1997, his younger sister, Astérie NIRERE (50), a farmer and widow of the late Léopold Rutebuka, and two of her children were executed in Nyamutera commune.
- On Thursday, 16 October 1997, between 7 a.m. and 8 a.m., RPA soldiers went to the home of Mrs. Généreuse HAKUZIMANA (59 years old), Major-General Déogratias Nsabimana's elder sister who lived with her husband in the Gashara cell, Ryinyo sector in NKULI commune, RUHENGERI prefecture. They ordered her to come out and accompany them to the small trading center of Bikingi, located at the bottom of the hill. There she was then ordered to kneel before she was executed on the spot by machine gun.

***

A few months later, my maternal grandparents suffered the same fate, also cowardly murdered by the RPA in their home in Karago, Gisenyi.

We were all sad. Mom was particularly devastated but had to stand up for us. She could never have imagined that we would experience another series of bereavements!

Barely a few months after reconnecting with her best friend, my godmother, Régine, died in Brussels under mysterious conditions. She and Mom had at least had time to themselves a few months after they had started playing teenagers again. So, when it was time to part after a visit, they accompanied each other, making the journeys on foot, until they decided that, all things considered, it was late and that it was better to sleepover either at one or the other's, depending on where the last journey had taken them.

About the same period, Didier left us, shortly after his best friend, the late Patrick, son of Patricia and Martin, our longtime friends.

Then it was Mom's great friend who lost her life following a cardiac arrest. Poor Béatrice had been separated from her husband during the war. But, like Mom, she had bravely raised her children on her own, with dignity, until the unthinkable happened in the early 2000s. She lost her son Patrick who perished in the prime of life in a car crash.

We buried our relatives, at least those we could accompany in Belgium. For others who died in Rwanda or in refugee camps, we had no option but to light candles and pray for them. In our tradition, one of the ways of mourning is to bury our loved ones to allow them to transition into the afterlife. We unfortunately did not even have the privilege of accompanying Dad to his final resting place, nor any of our aunts or grandparents, as we could have done if we still had a "home." Dad, who had built a family vault in our residence of Ndera, in the middle of nature, was not even entitled to a proper burial.

For years (and still today sometimes, I admit), we all dreamed of Dad alive, having escaped death and telling us that he had to hide so as not to compromise his family's safety. We still harbor the hope that one day we will be able to find his remains and organize a burial ceremony to finally close the circle.

We ended up living with this lack of ritual. While people buy flowers to embellish the graves of their loved ones once a year, we have contented ourselves, during all these years, with lighting a candle, saying a prayer, and changing our social profile pictures in remembrance.

CHAPTER IV

Reconstruction

The idea of telling our family history began to spring up in my mind as a duty of memory while we were in Bukavu in April 1994. I began by writing a few notes here and there. Then, for years, I let the idea mature. In addition to being caught up in the whirlwind of life, writing meant for me, each time, to immerse myself in this painful chapter that I did not necessarily want to reopen.

As I talked to my brothers and sisters later in the 2000s, I realized everyone wanted to share memories, pay tribute to our parents' teachings, and allow our father to speak through us. Yvonne, the most pious among us, had even had a kind of revelation. She sensed that we should carry Dad's message of peace, which he had not had time to complete before his untimely death.

It was not easy to exorcise all our memories in this way. Still, we tried to relate the facts as we experienced them with our impressions as growing children, teenagers, or adults. Each of us has done vital inner work to approach their reconstruction. We kept notes along the way and recorded, consciously or not, a smell, a sensation, which revived these images engraved forever in our memories.

We have chosen to relate our journey and conclude with some life lessons that have contributed to our rebirth and impacted our personal and professional choices.

1. Prayer

During our relocation to Europe, we did not place a high priority on consulting psychotherapists. However, given the hardships experienced, it would have been important, even essential, to use their services. Furthermore, Rwandan culture considers that the family unit and our friendly nature prevent us from sinking into depression. We, therefore, had to find other ways to overcome our suffering, starting with the therapeutic power of prayer, which comforted us in the face of events that continued to affect us.

Of my brothers and sisters, Yvonne had shown visible signs of trauma since we arrived in Belgium. She, who had always been pious since early childhood, was no longer so because she was angry with God. Yvonne wondered a lot about the meaning of life and concluded that no God loved her. Because if He existed, He would never have allowed us to endure all this, Dad's death, and her leaving everything behind to find herself lost in a new country that she had not chosen. God would not have let all those innocent people die in vain. No God would have allowed hatred to spread, allowing like-minded people to kill each other in the wildest way possible. She was consumed from within.

When she failed to find answers to why we had to go through these events, she put her relationship with God on hold until she became interested in Mormonism.[1] She

---

1. Mormon theology is the doctrine of The Church of Jesus Christ of Latter-day Saints. This doctrine includes the Plan of God also called the Plan of Happiness, the Plan of Redemption and the Plan of Salvation which consists in the fact that our existence in mortality has a purpose.

will never forget that first time she experienced the descent of the Spirit. This prompted her to learn the teachings of the missionary sisters. Then she read the *Book of Mormon*, focusing on the part about the wars between the Lamanites and the Nephites: how they fought and decided to make peace. This echoed what was happening in Rwanda. She saw a metaphor between the Tutsis and the Hutus through these two nations. She then saw that peace could be possible among Rwandans one day, thanks to the Gospel!

The teachings and hymns gradually opened her heart, which had hardened and darkened from negative feelings caused by fear, depression, hatred, doubt, despair, and trauma. She finally began to find answers: if God was alive, He could wipe away her tears and allay her fears. She understood that God did not hate her and had not abandoned her. Then, Yvonne took on the work of self-forgiveness for being too hard on herself. All the anger she had built up inside her started to crumble away. She, who had even considered suicide as a way out, now opened her heart. By letting go of all her rage, she realized she was not the only one who suffered. Following this, she believes that she developed the true love of Christ towards others by also forgiving those who took our father's life and family members. She found her only true therapy in the Gospel, bringing her answers and inner peace and helping her become a being filled with compassion towards others. Finally, she understood the meaning of the words that Jesus Christ spoke before taking his last breath: *Father, forgive them for they do not know what they are doing.* Thanks to her, prayer has regained its place at home, bringing peace to each of us, and we are grateful to her.

For me, it was a very sad event that pushed me to come back to pray assiduously. In June 1995, the tragic disappearance of little Julie and Mélissa, barely eight years old, completely shocked me. I was only eighteen then and becoming a mother one day was still a distant yet certain hypothesis. In my student apartment, I recall listening to newscasters announce a few months after their disappearance that their little bodies had been found four meters deep in Sars-la-Buissière, in the house of the most notorious pedophile in the country. I cried a lot for these little princesses who died at the dawn of their lives and prayed for their parents, for my future children, so that God would preserve them.

2. Perseverance

When Dad died, Mom taught us very early on to project ourselves into the future, to be strong, to dream, and, above all, to act. I have always found Mom very modern and well ahead of her time. By reading all the teachings around well-being that exist today, I realize that she has always pushed us to practice what is often called the law of attraction. She kept telling us that we had to visualize what we wanted and that we could accomplish what we wanted if we put the necessary energy into it. My social integration in Belgium was greatly facilitated by this life lesson.

After finishing my secondary education in the summer of 1996, I moved into a small apartment in Etterbeek, in the building where my sister Denise already lived. I had to make it on my own, especially since we were cramped in our social housing in Jette. In my opinion, being able to occupy 50 square meters (or about 538 square feet) alone was a real luxury. What's more, having just turned nineteen, I was confident and excited to embark on a new chapter in my life.

I had also drawn up a budget, following Dad's example. He was so organized that he left almost nothing to chance.

Each year, starting in January, he liked to gather our family to discuss the upcoming year's plans in advance, including the summer vacations. His discipline, certainly linked to his military training, is the main quality I proudly inherited and that marked us all.

After receiving the equivalent of nine hundred euros that I expected to receive from the Public Center for Social Action (Centre public d'action sociale, CPAS), I would have enough left over to live comfortably after paying the three hundred and fifty euros in rent. So I enrolled at the Free University of Brussels (Université libre de Belgique, ULB) to start a degree in political science. In parallel, I registered with the CPAS, which took a long time to process my file before finally denying me financial aid because this money was not intended to fund higher education. On the other hand, they were ready to provide me with food aid. Once a week, I could go collect food. Having found this decision unfair, I appealed, but they confirmed I was only entitled to receive food. So I would not be able to continue at the university. I had to find an emergency solution.

I still went to class every morning, but my heart was not in it. Already, I found it difficult to focus with at least two hundred other students! I tried moving to the front rows to follow more easily. The transition from high school to university was not at all easy. No one was there to give us a learning method. As the saying goes, "every man for himself, God for all."

So, the first time I went to look for food at the CPAS, I came back with boxes of goulash (a mix of canned meat and vegetables) and ravioli in jars. I tried them the same evening and never went back afterward. Since early childhood, I was used to eating *homemade* food with fresh ingredients straight out of our pesticide-free vegetable garden. And even with our limited means, Mom went to the market every Sunday to stock up on fresh produce that we consumed at home, except for certain ends of the month when we had to make do with *fricadelles* and ravioli. Suffice it to say that the switch to tin cans was simply insurmountable.

After a few months, I understood that it was impossible to continue to claim money from Mom, and I was completely broke. My sisters and I had our customers for the braids, but it was not enough to pay the rent and the food, the only expenses I could afford. I would also like to thank my former landlord of rue de la Duchesse for trusting me by granting me credit for a few months.

As I did not want to backtrack and return home, I had to give in to the pressure to register with the Brussels Regional Employment Office (ORBEM). The professional guidance counselors, who were very friendly, helped me write a curriculum vitae and quickly found me a job as an executive secretary in an association organizing operettas at the Cultural Center of Woluwe-Saint-Pierre. I thus had to abandon my first year of university at the ULB to start working, but it was only a postponement. I registered for evening classes in the same academic stream at Saint-Louis University for the next school year in September.

For two years, I combined a full-time job with my candidacy studies.[2] It was difficult because of the rhythm I had to sustain. I worked from nine to five during the day, then continued with evening classes from six to nine in the week and some Saturday mornings. I was quickly losing steam at this pace. Moreover, the professional environment in

---

2. Before the Bologna decree of 2004, which established a three-year bachelor's education system, the university degree in most subjects was obtained in four years: two years of candidacy, two years of license.

which I worked, our basement-based office, and Woluwe-Saint-Pierre's town hall bell, which rang every hour, did not appeal to me. The bell still echoes in my head when I take my daughters to the municipal library. But never mind, I met great people at my work and Saint-Louis and paid my rent arrears.

In May 2000, the nonprofit I worked for was liquidated, offering employees the possibility of unemployment benefits if they did not find a job immediately. The agenda coincided perfectly because I was completing my application for Saint-Louis. So, I asked if I could benefit from an exemption from clocking in for two years to continue my last two years in daytime classes. When my request was granted, it felt like sweet revenge on life.

So, I continued my degree in International Relations at the ULB. I had to get used to the rhythm of being a "daytime" student again and learn to manage the concerns of young people my age. We were not very fond of the hazing tradition, like most African students at ULB. However, it amused us to see the young people come and drop their pants to show off their behinds in front of the audience or disguise themselves in ridiculous clothes by clowning around to get some change. Fortunately, the teachers clearly explained the excesses that could result from this. They left us the freedom to take part or not, making us understand that we had to be present in class, given that this tradition was not necessarily a guarantee of integration. I had great encounters and made friends for life with whom I still meet and continue to share good times. Here's to you my ULB friends: Magali, Kally, Aimable, Pitchou, Mylène, Maryse, Lydie, Éline, Maxime, Éric ...

After getting my degree, I did what society expected of me, which I naturally found to be the right path. I worked in the headline programming department for a few months at the Belgian Radio-Television of the Wallonia-Brussels Federation (RTBF). It's a place that I liked because I often saw TV hosts.

I then worked for a few months at Fortis Bank, managing stock options. It was not really a job I felt comfortable in. In addition, I endured an ignorant and racist colleague who kept saying I was lucky to be in Belgium. He would compare Africa to "a small country where people live in a primitive manner." He thought the whole continent comprised houses perched in the trees. Children walked around barefoot, collecting water from the wells, and foraging branches to light fires! To top it off, one day he suggested I dress up for carnival like Josephine Baker with a belt made of bananas. I learned at that time the power of my gaze, this famous characteristic of the Nsabimanas. Later, he told me that I had flashed him with my eyes. Fortunately, I never saw him again after completing this assignment.

As the days went on, life continued with all the good things it could offer, such as moments shared with family and friends. I finally had enough money to buy new clothes and shoes. Yet, the frequent dark news about Rwanda and my first broken heart made me experience less good times, as did many other young adults.

One evening, out with my friends, I ran into the man who was to become my husband. Traumatized by the murderous madness that had gripped some of my compatriots, I still could not imagine marrying a Rwandan. Boney comes from Cameroon. He often tells me that in my misfortune, there was this part of luck because he would never have met me if there had not been a war in Rwanda. He's probably right since my path had been mapped out. Thanks to him, I have a third nation, Cameroon. His native region,

Kumbo, in the northwest, strangely resembles Rwanda with its red soils, mild climate, and exotic fruits.

As time evolved, I had the feeling of resuming a normal course of life. My perseverance was finally starting to pay off.

Later, I made Mom proud and happy once again by giving her grandchildren. She had expressed her wish to have many descendants. In Kinyarwanda, the supreme compliment that one can receive, especially as newlyweds, is: *"Muzabyare muheke,"* which means "May you have children and carry them on your back."

3. Personal Development

For Fabrice, life also took a different turn. He confronted his trauma at some later point in his career. When we arrived in Belgium, he had to work hard to learn French to communicate with his classmates.

Later, when he was starting high school, it was basketball that forged his character. In his spare time, he spent hours dribbling at Jette Youth Park and watching basketball star Michael Jordan. Meanwhile, Fabrice secretly dreamt of playing for the National Basketball Association (NBA), America's premier basketball league. But to get there, he understood that he had to stretch his limits. It did not matter whether it was snowing, windy, or raining, as is customary in Belgium. He never missed a training session.

However, in his teens, around sixteen, we noticed that he began to feel bad about himself. He had lost motivation for his studies. Then, he started hanging out with friends who, like him, were school dropouts. After being kicked out of school, he felt like he'd hit rock bottom, shattering all his determination and the discipline he had forged with basketball.

Dad had died when Fabrice was barely nine years old. He had not been able to express his feelings about what he had gone through. With the war trauma resurfacing, he blamed himself, wondering why he had survived when some of his friends had not. The sounds, smells, and fragrances of flowers brought back memories of Rwanda and the corpses spread across the streets when we were evacuated. To avoid facing the reality of his situation, he turned to alcohol as an escape. As he did when we arrived in Belgium in 1994, he started having nightmares again, describing seeing soldiers shooting at us.

After failing his fifth year of high school (eleventh grade) for a second time, he hit rock bottom. That day in late June, he came home and broke down crying, disappointed that he had failed again. His future was at risk. As a result, he had to decide whether or not to get up and embark on a long reconstruction journey. Several mentors got him back on track, including Maurice, our brother, who sparked his interest in reading, and Cherif Ousmane Aidara, the Senegalese teacher, who gave him private lessons every night of the week, repeating his favorite credo "in war as in war."

After a year of hard work, he passed his Jury Central exams, allowing him to complete his secondary school education in one year instead of two. Mom and Maurice sat breathless on graduation day. Fabrice had secretly kept this premonitory dream to himself: his name would resound in the amphitheater among the successful. He waited with his eyes closed, finally hearing his name: "Fabrice Nsabimana." He had just earned his admission ticket to college. He thanked God for supporting him in his hard work.

Finally, his efforts paid off, and he told himself that if he was lucky enough to be alive, it would be precisely to find a purpose and honor all those lives lost in vain. In his view, time is the only cure; what did not kill him simply made him stronger, as this famous phrase puts it so eloquently. His character was forged by his brush with death and his experience at rock bottom.

With Mom's blessing, he left to build a new life in the United States. There, he again encountered clashes of cultures and bouts of racism, leading him to question his identity. Following a few alcoholic drifts and determined not to sink further, he began to read again. The phrase "Whatever the mind can conceive and believe, it can achieve" was adopted by him from Napoleon Hill's *Think and Grow Rich*. Whenever he faced a new challenge, such as becoming a father for the first time, he redefined his goals and told himself that he would achieve them.

With the help of self-discipline, training, and readings on spirituality and motivation, he continues to develop his personal growth. Furthermore, he can rely on the love of his wife Sariah and children and the support of his friends and family.

4. Perspective

Since that fateful day of April 6, 1994, Denise seemed to be living like an automaton, burying her feelings deep within. I only became aware of the extent of her trauma after listening to her voice recordings. After Dad's death, she said she went through a period of deep questioning, wondering why and how it all happened. Why did our Rwandan compatriots become so cruel to one another? She could not find any concrete answers to this question, preferring to use a philosophical approach instead. Finally, she concluded that what happened was guided by a force beyond our control, which teaches us and distinguishes between good and evil, and that within every individual, there is a part of God and a part of the devil that guides their behavior. Her analysis satisfied her, so she pursued the path she had been offered.

In 2009, however, she went through a rough period, and her demons finally caught up with her. She had let herself be carried away by the whirlwind of life by burying her suffering and her lack of bearings as much as possible. Happy events such as the end of her education, her marriage, the birth of her first child, and a job she found easily were followed by other less fortunate events: her divorce, and her life as an expatriate synonymous with isolation in a golden cage. Since she changed countries frequently, she had never been able to settle down and reflect on her life. Instead, she felt as though she were sailing on a river without being able to stop the rudderless boat, advancing without guidance.

Eventually, when burnt out, everything exploded in her face, and she reached the breaking point. While living in Douala, Cameroon, she ran out of steam and decided to put her career on hold. In the fifteen years following the event that completely altered the course of her life, she realized that she had never mourned. Instead, she was experiencing even greater pain because she still lacked answers to all the questions she had asked herself a few years earlier.

To recharge her batteries with her family, she needed to return home. Since Belgium was her safe haven, she packed her bags and moved back to Brussels. Despite not understanding the psychological torture she underwent, I was delighted to see her return. However, when the dust settled, the film of her life resurfaced: she realized that despite what she had foreseen, she did not feel at home here either. Her neighbors in the municipality of Dilbeek spoke Flemish, a language she did not yet speak. This was not the peace she had expected to find by going back.

She told me that she had had the courage to consult with a psychologist, who she believed could help her get out of this black hole and teach her how to solve the puzzle of her life. The work was focused on her identity crisis, on her inability to comprehend how her life had been turned upside down by the sudden death of her father. The therapy taught her to build a little cocoon wherever she was and to stop viewing "home" as a geographical concept. Thus, she became aware that if she could return to Rwanda, she would not necessarily feel at home there since she would find neither Dad nor her house there, nor her friends, nothing of this old life she had left. This capsule simply no longer existed.

As a result, she decided to make a radical change and return to her childhood passions. She had always secretly wished to work with her hands in a job allowing her to do so. In order to make her dream come true, she undertook a degree in aesthetics, which enabled her to meet people who had experienced somewhat similar or difficult circumstances. Many of the students already had a past, sometimes heavy as well. They were trying to reorient themselves in order to find meaning in their lives. It was a very different environment from ICHEC, where she had lived relatively carefree and with some confidence in the future, surrounded by people who shared similar ambitions.

She nonetheless had one thing to accomplish. Over time, she developed a secret obsession with returning to Rwanda, as if she had to walk on our red soil to complete the puzzle of her life. Finally, in December 2012, that dream came true. She told us about it. Although we were afraid for her, we respected her desire and understood that dissuading her was pointless.

She traveled with apprehension. She feared being stared at, arrested upon landing, or identified. However, none of that occurred. Her peers, in contrast, shared the same language, culture, and cuisine (bland, compared to our African neighbors, it must be admitted). So, when she found herself in a lodge in Ruhengeri, admiring the Sabyinyo Volcano as we used to do with Grandmother, who loved to watch the scenery while smoking her pipe, sitting atop the hill, she experienced a tremendous sense of peace, fullness, and serenity.

This trip had a significant impact on her mental health. She was surprised to discover that the ticking that had consumed her for almost twenty years had ceased. Although her trip to Rwanda did not provide her with answers to what had occurred, it nevertheless gave her a chance to immerse herself in many things, especially positive ones, and regain a new sense of purpose. By closing the loop, Denise could finally look at the future differently.

Her hard work ethic, righteousness, and openness to the world are traits she inherited from our parents. But, as harsh as their parenting once seemed, it has taken on a whole new meaning and turned out to be a lifeline when she most needed it.

As a result of her open-mindedness, she encourages us to position ourselves as global citizens.

5. Purpose

Schooling also went well for Josiane on the surface, but she was still traumatized and scarred by the war. As a result, she had difficulty finding her place in secondary school. When Mom realized she was losing her footing, she decided to change schools to find a school she would enjoy. As a result, she successfully completed her secondary education.

Stylist at heart, she chose to join the Francisco Ferrer Institute of Arts and Crafts. But even though she excelled in these subjects, she was still unable to find meaning in her life. Because of the events in Rwanda, she carried a great deal of anger within her. The once calm little girl had transformed into a lioness ready to bite at every corner. And like Fabrice, she found a comforting companion in alcohol. Of all of us, she's the one who really inherited Dad's piercing gaze, something even more pronounced after half a bottle of wine.

Seeing that she was sinking deeper and deeper, Mom sent her to Romania, hoping Denise, who had moved to Bucharest for professional reasons, could help her to regain meaning to her life by welcoming her into her home and helping her change her environment. But, above all, Josiane was looking for her destiny.

Romania was a winning plan; she successfully completed her education in business administration. There, she discovered a culture and an atmosphere that she describes as warm and welcoming, similar to African values. In addition, her artistic nature led her to quickly find a dance company that allowed her to perform at concerts featuring Romanian celebrities. Finally, Romania's authentic back country, without electricity, reminded her of our childhood visits to our grandparents in Gisenyi and Ruhengeri.

With her Romanian companion, Alexandru, who would become her husband a few years later, she returned from Romania completely transformed, warm, and fulfilled. She regained her sparkle and was ready to face the world again.

It was not hard for her to find her place on "the Boulevard," the so-called Louise district of Brussels, with its luxury boutiques, thanks to her natural style, volubility, and fluency in languages (she was now fluent in Romanian and English). Within a short period, she advanced from sales to positions of responsibility as an assistant and artistic director.

She was still contemplating her fate. A fashionista at heart, she wondered how she could combine her love for fashion with her desire to give back to society what she had received. So she founded her clothing brand *Muhire*, which is also her second Rwandan name and means luck, in 2017, inspired by Peter Drucker's quote, "You cannot predict the future, but you can create it."

Since a young age, Josiane has been fascinated with art and the world of fashion design. With the support of her brand, she intends to establish a foundation that will provide access to design education for the most disadvantaged. She considers art and artistic expression around clothing to be more than just beauty for the sake of beauty, but as a means of bringing people together around the universal value of love.

Josiane is a model of resilience. She works tirelessly, putting Afro-European aesthetics to music, thanks to her know-how learned in the world of luxury, but also from Belgian and Romanian craftsmen.

She is a great source of inspiration for me. Despite difficulties and discouragements, she maintains her course.

6. Forgiveness

Maurice, our eldest sibling, who is supposed to have more experience than us all, has always been one step ahead regarding forgiveness. It was very clear to him from the start that we are not the only ones to have faced being refugees, along with all of the emotional and material difficulties that it entails. He served as president of the African Students Union in Graz, Austria, during the early 1990s, which brought together political refugees from all walks of life, including Rwandan Tutsis and other African immigrants. He and his comrades interceded on behalf of the asylum seekers with the authorities to facilitate the process. In 1994, when our family needed assistance with our administrative procedures, he could assist us easily with this experience.

His empathy enabled him to help people cope with difficult events, even if he had never been through them. At their side, he was able to pragmatically address various issues, including the issue of social integration. The serious car accident he suffered in Rwanda two years earlier had led him to embrace the notion of gratitude, convinced that the only way to be grateful to be alive is to do good around him.

Maurice evidently felt the pain that a son can experience when Dad passed away. After the plane was shot down on April 6, 1994, he experienced a moment of anger and hatred. Nevertheless, he regained his composure very quickly, analyzing the repercussions that this attack would have on the Rwandan population.

From Maurice's perspective, every Rwandan has been traumatized by our country's dark history, experiencing the loss of a loved one. There was, however, a choice between perpetuating this chain of causality to regain one's peace at the expense of others, which may increase and maintain suffering, or doing good around oneself without necessarily waiting for all others to reach the same state of mind.

He chose the path of forgiveness since he believed that no human being fundamentally seeks to harm another and that those who do so perpetuate the suffering they experience within themselves. Everyone has suffered losses in their lives as part of a continuum of suffering. It is a chain that can be perpetuated indefinitely if refugees nurture the desire to return violently and Rwandans commit crimes against one another.

Several years earlier, Dad had already instilled in him these notions of forgiveness and compassion towards others. Indeed, our father distinguished himself in the war that began in Rwanda in 1990 by bravely defending his country against an invasion by the RPF. Taking casualties among his men was certainly not easy. Not an easy task to kill either, since behind every fighter stood a mother, a wife, or a sister who had lost a loved one. During the summer of 1993, Dad told Maurice that he had been trained in warfighting and felt confident regarding military strategy. But what he had not expected was to come face-to-face with weapons-wielding children. The issue of child soldiers affected many African armies, as well as the RPF. Although a battlefield is certainly not comparable to a competition between two opposing teams on a football field, I frequently heard Dad saying that a war does not make winners because the losses on the human level affect each party and that real peace among Rwandans could only be achieved through the implementation of the Arusha peace accords. Furthermore, I recall laughing nervously in 1993 when Dad announced, with stoic calm and without bitterness, that Major Kagame would become the Deputy Chief of Staff following the merger of the two armies.

It was only a few years later that we understood, thanks to Maurice, that our father had forgiven himself and had found a deep peace, undoubtedly offering him the possibility of feeling empathy for his opponents. But, after all, if he wanted to retire within five years, when he reached the age of fifty-five, he had to hurry to bring about the merger of the Rwandan Armed Forces and the Rwandan Patriotic Army, the RPF's armed wing.

As a result of these reflections, we have discussed the issues of forgiveness, mutual understanding, and empathy as siblings. It has helped us to calmly approach these notions by telling ourselves that we are equal in the eyes of God, regardless of the name we choose for Him or the philosophy we follow. This was the first step. Therefore, as our parents taught us, seeing others as less important or significant implies that we do not believe that God can love them equally. Hence the importance of cultivating a love for one's neighbor.

In fact, it is very easy to hate people because they are different from us. This is how racism takes root. In Rwanda, what happened is racism between two ethnic groups. Unlike our neighbors in Congo, Ghana, Cameroon, and elsewhere, where there are a multitude of tribes, languages, and customs, our country has only three ethnic groups that share the same language, culture, and overall customs.

As individuals raised with respect for human beings and a spirit of openness, we have developed an ability to listen to others and not focus primarily on our history and concerns.

Thus, I recently read the book *Petit pays* by Gaël Faye in one sitting. This shook me to the core and made me cry because it tells the story from the other side of the looking glass; that is to say, from the perspective of Rwandans who had fled and did not feel welcome at home or in the country where they were now living, Burundi, in this case. Ultimately, they won the country by war. Still, after so much suffering, the victory left a bitter taste in the mouths of those who had lost a large portion of their family.

Currently, we are seen as the "others," as if history is about to repeat itself. But is this what the future requires?

Hopefully, all those who have experienced these atrocities will say to themselves: never again. Our hope is that we will have the opportunity to shake hands to symbolize forgiveness and fraternity and that we may even be able to unite these factions, which persist in maintaining their positions because they have remained locked in their hatred for a long time, perhaps because they have been unable to grieve before being able to forgive.

Perhaps Rwandans will change our hearts permanently if we break this cycle of violence in which we have been mired for generations. Quite simply, what has been going on for years is nothing more than a vicious circle: people killing families whose children then kill their opponents' children in retaliation. In Rwanda and throughout the world, this cycle must be permanently broken. Could one of the solutions be to join forces to end the cycle of hatred and war, choosing forgiveness as the best path leading to compassion, inner peace, and interdependence? From sympathy to empathy, then to compassion, we can see the other as a whole being with a right to exist and to have their own perspectives and opinions.

Exactly twenty-five years after our father disappeared, we wanted to convey this same message of tolerance to the Rwandan diaspora on April 6, 2019:

"Dear Dad,

Today, we honor you and thank you for your sacrifice. You have accomplished your mission on earth by serving your country and your family. The peace that illuminated your eyes remains with us to this very day since we know that you found it before leaving. Thank you and Mom for giving us the freedom of choice and thoughts, perseverance in hardship, fraternal support, and above all, the love of our neighbors regardless of their origin, ethnicity, skin color, social class, religion, or other differences."

7. Peace

I was honored to meet Mr. Johan Swinnen, who served as the Belgian Ambassador to Rwanda in 1994, and his wife at the end of 2018. Our initial discussion lasted hours. The point of view he presented was faithful and not necessarily tender towards the Rwandan authorities in charge between 1993 and 1994. It was refreshing to speak with him on an equal footing, and I was impressed by his charisma and respectability. He offered a great deal of wisdom and, most importantly, reflected what I think: "There is a lack of nuances in the Rwandan community."

What he described about Dad reinforced our image of him: a wise, thoughtful, honest, and above all, a moderate individual who deeply loved his country. In response to this meeting, I gained even greater energy and shared it with my brothers and sisters, choosing to carry a message of peace in our tales.

In addition, it was comforting to be reminded that we are also victims. Though we may be forgotten, we are victims, nonetheless. In the years following 1994, being Hutu has simply meant, especially for those who think simplistically, that we are "genocidaires" or negationists for expressing our pain as victims. It started very quickly, both in school and in the workplace. For years, as soon as we introduced ourselves as Rwandans the first question we were all confronted with was: "Ah, so you are part of the bad guys or good guys? With your features, we cannot say!" At first, this question was shocking and surprising, and I answered simply by stating that I am Rwandan. Full stop. However, at the same time, I was consumed by the feeling of shame and anger that I had to silence my story, which would undoubtedly be trivialized and would probably not confer enough suffering upon me to qualify as a victim. Therefore, my only option was to internalize and suffer in silence.

History cannot be rewritten, nor can facts be denied. The Rwandan presidential plane was shot down by missiles, the genocide against Tutsis did occur, and many people perished both before, as history has shown us, and after, especially in the camps in Zaire (today's Democratic Republic of the Congo) and Rwanda.

There are no "buts" that follow, no crimes that can justify others, and no extenuating circumstances are valid. In the same way, the victims must not replace or supplant each other. Every victim deserves respect, regardless of ethnicity or nationality.

In my mind, however, the question of lasting peace persists.

If we do not know who murdered our father, can we ever find peace? To date, the circumstances of the attack have not been established by a court of law. We will wait as long as necessary for the judicial authorities to shed light on this terrorist act.

Can our elders experience this peace? Unfortunately, our parents' generation is gradually dying off in their host countries before they can return to their motherland. At the same time, the younger generation wonders why they have not visited Rwanda yet?

Reconciliation seems far away when I follow Rwandan news or consult social media networks. Unfortunately, extremists on both sides continue to promote hatred by establishing a hierarchy of victims. However, there is a glimmer of hope: mentalities slowly change, a sign that history cannot continue transmitting one paradigm.

As if "enough is enough," we are all gradually but surely striving toward the same goal. Therefore, we hope that a unity process will begin with those who intend to move forward, who have forgiven and seek a way to live together tomorrow in Rwanda or elsewhere. Therefore, rather than positioning myself as a passive victim, I decided to act.

Due to my position in the middle of the family, I have always been the provider and receiver of both good and bad news. For most of my life, I have been consulted when conflicts arise or have asked for other people's advice. However, it also earned me the distinction of always being the one that is mentioned. If one of my brothers or sisters was not listening, it was obviously because I had influenced them! In summary, I decided to use my capacity to listen and to believe those who find interest in my person, to be their quiet rock, a source of strength, and a "person of confidence" within the workplace. At the same time, I decided to train in mediation because I am convinced that dialogue is the key to resolving conflicts.

Likewise, I hope to provide emotional security to those who turn to me, so they can express themselves freely and choose what is best for them. My dream is one day to facilitate the advancement of dialogue between Rwandans who aspire only to peace, as Dad did during his life, although his mission was unfortunately cut short.

Taking inspiration from Burundians or South Africans may help us achieve lasting peace among Rwandans. They have done this by establishing "Commission(s) for truth, justice, reparation, and reconciliation," in which every word is important to understand and acknowledge each other's suffering.

The country has made some welcome efforts, but will they be sufficient in the long run? Moreover, what plans do the Rwandan authorities have to integrate and unite all Rwandans? How can every Rwandan live in a fulfilling way and feel welcome at home?

It is to this inclusive Rwanda that we hope one day to bring our children, accompany our father's body to his homeland for burial, and gather at the graves of our relatives ...

Conclusion

U nimaginable violence can be heard in the accounts made by friends or others whose relatives lost their lives during the genocide against the *Tutsis* in 1994. The same can be said about the accounts made by our cousins who describe the savage executions of our relatives by members of the Rwandan Patriotic Army or their journey to refugee camps in former Zaire, where many died from cholera or dysentery.

With some friends, we have exchanged condolences and expressed our mutual compassion, each of us having paid a heavy price.

We understand that we share a common denominator, namely the suffering, because blood has no color, ethnicity, or nationality. Essentially, this notion of equality in pain means that we have the right and moral obligation to look forward to a peaceful future.

My observations of the Rwandan problem and participation in forgiveness circles inspired me to create "circles of resilience."

Why resilience? Because it is through our reconstruction that we will achieve the acceptance of others. Rwandan forums illustrate how there is still, unfortunately, a strong sense of polarization and distrust among the various groups.

In the same manner that we share a common culture and language, the victims also share a common pain, namely the inability to respect mourning rituals that have been dear to our tradition of accompanying our dead. Justice was provided to some, but is it sufficient to alleviate their heartache?

Every Rwandan has a story based on his or her own experience, which deserves to be heard and respected, as this is essential to achieving inner peace, in my opinion. Is it possible to spread this peace to others so that it becomes contagious?

The purpose of these circles, which are discussion groups, is to bring together individuals willing to share a common experience in complete freedom while respecting each other's narrative. The only requirement is to adhere to the disciplinary charter: respect for others and refrain from judging them.

Resilience circles are not therapeutic groups, however. Health professionals exist to treat mental disorders. Additionally, they do not have a punitive purpose. No blame can be placed on a person based on his story, losses, or feelings. Finally, they do not promote stigmatization or victimization of a group.

We have adopted this exercise as a mental shower for a small group. An example of openness to the world can be found in our immediate family. As siblings, we often joke that Dad would turn over in his grave (if he had one!), seeing that he now has grandchildren from the United States, Ghana, Congo, Cameroon, El Salvador, Romania, and Switzerland! The diversity of cultures has allowed us to see life differently, with people who do not necessarily see life the same way but live in harmony and respect one another. As a result of this perspective and a model of cosmopolitan living, we live every day intending to love our neighbor and achieve peace for all.

Among our siblings, we have chosen to adopt a lifestyle based on two values: universal love and the *spirit of Ubuntu.*[1] We are proud to share this love that has united us and enabled us to accomplish this. Despite our very deep wounds, speaking with each other and maintaining our fraternal friendship has allowed us to keep a healthy spirit and continue working on this project together. These bonds are perpetuated and passed on to our children, who love to meet up with their cousins. It is our moral obligation to go the extra mile for these grandchildren.

Completing this book took nearly three decades because, in addition to subjecting ourselves to the difficult exercise of remembering, we had different and ambivalent feelings regarding the need to expose ourselves. Despite fears of politicization and trivialization, we needed a driving force to motivate us to take action.

Based on our father's daily experience with us, his personal notes, his memoirs, and his stories, but also on the testimonies of those who knew him, we were able to reassemble certain pieces of the puzzle to draw a faithful portrait of Dad, a key player during the Rwandan crisis from 1990 to 1994.

Admittedly, our trajectory is no longer the same as before April 6, 1994. Yet, despite this, we continue to approach life with serenity and hope for the future. We are grateful to have found a country of welcome that allows us to practice the most rewarding job in the world, that

1. *Ubuntu* is an African and humanistic philosophy which consists in advocating the action of the good towards the others. These acts of benevolence are profitable both for the individual and for his or her community.

of being parents, in complete safety. And we hope that our children's children will find their place wherever their hearts lead them and that they will be able to proudly claim their Nsabimana heritage for generations to come.

Afterword

Almost everyone has heard of the Rwandan genocide that occurred in 1994, in which an estimated 800,000 people, Tutsis in majority, Hutus and Twas, were killed. That being said, few have shared their own story of being intimate witnesses to the events happening in Rwanda both before and after the assassination of the President of Rwanda, Juvénal Habyarimana, and the President of Burundi, Cyprien Ntaryamira, both Hutus, when the Rwandan presidential plane was shot down on April 6. It also killed Major General Déogratias Nsabimana, Chief of Staff of the Rwandan Armed Forces, and several other officials. This tragedy left a power vacuum that ultimately led to the Rwandan genocide.

Through her and her siblings' personal stories, Alice Nsabimana, daughter of Major General Nsabimana, gives us an insight into Rwandan life before and during the war and how her father and President Habyarimana worked tirelessly to achieve lasting peace in Rwanda. She shares with us not only an intimate portrait of her father and the terrifying events soon after the tragedy involving her family's escape from Rwanda and how she and her siblings' life dramatically changed as they fled Rwanda, becoming refugees and part of the Rwandan diaspora. It is a story of resilience and survival but, more importantly, of forgiveness and compassion that allowed her family to move forward in their own lives and heal.

James R. Doty, M.D.
Adjunct Professor
Founder & Director, The Center for Compassion
and Altruism Research and Education
at Stanford University School of Medicine
New York Times bestselling author of *Into the Magic
Shop: A Neurosurgeon's Quest to Discover the Mysteries
of the Brain and the Secrets of the Heart*

Déogratias Nsabimana - Military Background

On August 1, 1966, he was admitted to the Rwandan Military Academy (Officers' School) in Kigali and graduated as head of promotion with the rank of second lieutenant in 1968.

In 1968, he was an instructor at the military training center in Butare, Rwanda.

He served as President Grégoire Kayibanda's aide-de-camp (Military Aide) from 1969 to early 1973.

In 1973, he joined the Royal Higher Institute for Defense, Belgium's highest military academic institute (cf. Defense College, previously War College), for Command and General Staff Officer training. He graduated with a "General Staff Brevet" (*Brevet d'état-major* or BEM in French) in 1975.

From 1975 to 1980, he served as Rwandan Military Attaché in Brussels, Belgium.

From 1980 to 1984, he was First Plenipotentiary Counselor at the Rwandan Embassy and Military Attaché in Tripoli, Libya.

Back in Rwanda in 1984, he was appointed second in command of the Ecole Supérieure Militaire (ESM) in Kigali.

In 1988, he was appointed commander of the Gako Military Training Center in Bugesera, eastern Rwanda.

In October 1990, after the Rwandan Patriotic Front's (RPF) attack, he was appointed commander of the operational sector of Mutara, the combat zone in northern Rwanda.

On June 10, 1992, he was appointed Chief of Staff of the Rwandan army.

In December 1993, he was promoted to major-general.

On February 10, 1994, he was appointed Officer of the Legion of Honor by the French President, Mr. François Mitterrand.

Déogratias Nsabimana died on April 6, 1994, aboard the presidential plane shot down by missiles in Kigali, Rwanda.

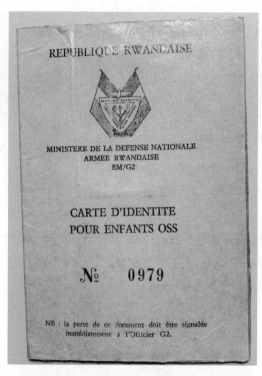

The officers' child ID card that saved my life.

June 1994, before leaving Bukavu. With Yvette,
who knew how to make me smile again.

Yvonne, captured in a moment of prayer.

Ever persevering, mom keeps smiling with Claudine
and Fabrice despite the appalling journey.

Fabrice in a natural environment
where he likes to recharge
his batteries.

Denise, in Ruhengeri, 2012

The fashionista born in our family, Josiane.

It is a message of peace and forgiveness that the Nsabimana siblings wished to deliver during the commemoration of April 6, 2019.

Mom and her grandchildren.

A big thank you to my brothers and sisters, Maurice, Denise, Yvonne, Josiane, and Fabrice: we are stronger together.

Major General BEM Déogratias Nsabimana
(23/08/1945 – 6/04/1994)

Among the few belongings and material memories
that we have left of Dad, we recovered the military insignia
and the pin that he wore on his military beret.

APPENDIX I

Personal Notes Taken by General Nsabimana between 8 December 1993 and 17 February 1994[1]

Meeting of 12/08/1993 in Ngondore

Update on meetings already held

Patrick (Mazimpaka)[2]'s statement

Issues that were the basis for the suspension of meetings:

- The incident of people arrested from Ndusu
  Message from the RPF after the resolution of the incident
  No reaction from the Rwandan government
- Later the Rwandan Ministry of Defense (MINADEF) declared that the talks were suspended, but the government did not officially announce the resumption

---

1. These notes were handwritten in French. The author and translator transcribed them and translated them into English. For the original French, please see *Résilience, Crise des grands lacs* by Alice Nsabimana (ISBN 978-2-8052-0727-3).
2. Patrick Mazimpaka (or Mazimhaka), the Second Vice Chair of the RPF and its principal negotiator

- Thanks to the United Nations Assistance Mission for Rwanda (UNAMIR), who did everything for the resumption of work; Commitment to the peace agreement
Rwandan government skipping agreements; the RPF does not know why.

My message

- Thanks
- No competence to address political-level issues
- Importance of the peace agreement but the role of the Rwandans themselves
- The Rwandan army seeks peace and appeals to the Rwandan Patriotic Front (RPF) to do the same

Intervention by Patrick

- Thanks
- The RPF abides by the peace agreement and wishes and is willing to do everything possible
- Think that the Rwandan Army (AR) is really committed to the path of peace.
- For him, the allegations conveyed by MINADEF no longer make sense, but allegations continue from certain authorities.
- UNAMIR is investigating - Rwanda will know the truth.

Intervention by the General (Dallaire[3])

- Letter from MINADEF on resumption of work in committee. It made it possible to initiate contacts with the RPF
- Basis of his work: Articles 54 and 79, paragraph 3[4].
- Regret over the absence of certain personalities, but late notice from UNAMIR could be the cause

---

3. Roméo Dallaire, Force Commander of UNAMIR, the ill-fated United Nations peacekeeping force for Rwanda between 1993 and 1994
4. Of the "Protocol of Agreement between the Government of the Republic of Rwanda and the Rwandese Patriotic Front on the Integration of the Armed Forces of the Two Parties"

- Decision to be taken cannot lack political impact
- Interpretation of Section 79[5]

Mazimpaka

Interpretation of violations: joint military commission

Work done so far: Disciplinary regulations, military regulations, statutes, operating principles of the National Gendarmerie[6]

Areas to explore: tactics, political and civic education, traffic police, (armament

Work done: disciplinary rules

Proposal by the General on the work of the Commission

What about UNAMIR's help in training? (not only a role of facilitator between the two armies)

Proposed program covers: disengagement, demobilization, integration, and evolution of the national army.

Study of the proposed document

From a common point of view: separate studies of the document and a proposal for its application

From the UNAMIR point of view:

Only two articles of the agreement define the role of UNAMIR

Work in a team of three

Another UNAMIR mandate if we refer to the ceasefire agreement

Create something between the program commission and the joint political-military commission

Create specific subgroups

Work in three: UNAMIR, Army Command, RPF

---

5. Idem
6. Rwanda's military force in charge of law enforcement

My point of view

Limited time given the magnitude of the task at hand, hence the creation of several sub-groups

General Dallaire

Also thought of a commission that would be responsible for studying the problem, which remains contentious

Resumes the work of the commission from Monday at 1 p.m. in Gondore at the end of the week

Mazimpaka

Establishment of the desired mixed politico-military commission as decided during the meeting of the President of the Republic and the President of the RPF (appoint the permanent members)

What about the RPF battalion's special training in Kigali, related to training in escort procedures

Privately

A. *Draft on letter for lack of collaboration*
    1. Tactical arrangement of forces (not yet provided) and weapons on the ground (Inform UNAMIR of changes -> movement, relief)
    2. Comments on security measures procedure in Kigali
    3. Site for the RPF battalion and dignitaries
    4. Response to the presence of foreign forces
    5. RPF letter on the security of RPF liaison officers in Kigali

B. *Security of the Ngondore area (withdraw the troops in the mountains and on the roadblock; wait for contact with the sector commanding officer)*

Frank collaboration with UNAMIR requested

MINADEF meeting on 12/13/1993

General information

A. *Last high-level meeting between the RPF and the Rwandan government under the chairmanship of UNAMIR was on December 9, 1993, in Kinihira.*

- Establishment of Broad-Based Transitional Government (GTBE) - no fixed date, but probably between 26 and 31 December 1993. Hence:
  - Urgent military files to update and forward to the government
  - Demobilization Commission to complete its work
  - Consignment of our secret documents (hide the radio operator)
- Spontaneous repatriation, in particular of Rwandan refugees settled in Burundi — position presented by the RPF and supported by the United Nations Development Program (UNDP) and the United Nations High Commissioner for Refugees (UNHCR)

B. *Domestic political situation*
- Coalition government inoperative
- Political party dissension
  - Efforts of the contact group to reunite (both wings of) the Democratic Republican Movement (MDR)
  - Congress of the Liberal Party (PL) (weekend of 12 to 13) but the PL party excluded from the Democratic Forces for Change (FDC).
  - Letter from the RPF declaring its refusal to participate in the Council of Government with the sole representation of Mugenzi's wing.

C. *Army Tract: probably written by the RPF*

D. *Departure of the French*
  - NOROIT Detachment left on December 11, 1993
  - Security in the city of Kigali (meeting coordinated with UNAMIR)

E. Insecurity in the country
Resumption of terrorism and armed banditry.

A committee composed of representatives of the Ministries concerned with security has been set up. MINADEF would be represented there by the 2 * G2

F. Starvation problem
There are already victims of hunger. The whole country has been affected (refugees - internally displaced persons)

G. Moving Kami camp
Clear Camp Kami by December 22. Quote for alternative camp relocation?

Review of the document entitled "Operational Procedure for the Establishment of the Kigali Weapons Storage Area":

Document saving

1. It is a question of organizing weapons control and not putting them under lock and key.
2. Provide our deployment (map) of forces and weapons in Kigali
3. Deployment plans to be presented by UNAMIR and RPF simultaneously
4. RPF battalion rotation plans to be provided

To do

1. Coordinate UNAMIR activities with the City Operational Sector Command + specify the mandate of the RPF
2. Security of the President of the Republic
3. Security in all other parts of the country
4. Prepare HCCA work group => G4

Study of the proposal for forming working groups

Scholarship problem

Relevance: need of the armed forces

Criteria (for all forces and all people): to be communicated before each course; avoid individual nominations as much as possible

FAR budget reduction measures

1. Abolition of the frontline (hazard) bonus (+- 600,000 million, or 2 months' salary)
2. Increase; notice: pay as promised, a bottle of beer
3. Removal of the ration
   Conclusion: Inopportune moment; national austerity hence all the ministries concerned, the particularity of the statute, superficial study.

MINADEF meeting on 12/14/1993

1. Security mechanism in the city of Kigali
2. Stakeholder coordination
3. Open item
4. Follow-up from the Ngondore meeting

Intervention of General Dallaire

Implementation of the GTBE: in principle before the end of the year, hence the implementation of the consignment area as of December 20, 1993.

Agenda

Discussion on the document proposed by UNAMIR

Kanyamanza: work desk for the pilots of the Belgian team at the airport

Avoid

Concept => paralysis

Threat from the city of Kigali => RPF office; infiltration, troops

Deployment of observers to Mulindi; sensitive goals

Deployment of troops and fires

- To be provided/submitted at the meeting of the 15th at MINADEF (Muberuka)
- Succession plan
- Kigali city map (vital points)

Foreign troops

Specify the nature of their role in Rwanda to assess how they could contribute to the training of the two armies

Official Journal of August 15, 1993

- Setback Distance to Ngondore
- May agreement on simultaneous withdrawal RPF-RGF; Thursday morning at 10 a.m. in Ngondore => G3. Departure from the UNAMIR at 9 a.m.
- Mixed commissions

Agreed

Deputy to Lieutenant-Colonel BEM Rwabalinda

Send document on UNAMIR proposal to MINADEF

MINADEF meeting on 12/21/1993

Participants

Army Command - UNAMIR

Topics

Camp security

Airport

Monitoring RPF battalion

Territorial defense during the disengagement: Prepare a working document

Debates

- Camp security: plan for sufficient numbers
- Airport: review the concept of defense
- Regulation of outings of RPF soldiers during normal hours of service: escort *UNAMIR* Identification
- When to Proceed to Execution of Section 15A, Measures for FPR Relocation
- RPF remark on the consignment zone
- Installation of RPF battalion (600 people, weapons, ammunition)

12/22/1993 - Army Command meeting

Object: Operational procedure for the establishment of the weapons storage area in Kigali

A document produced at UNAMIR's initiative and subject to counterproposals from the Rwandan side. It still needs to be finalized this morning to include defense measures for sensitive locations

How to understand the document

Fits within the peace processes recommended by the Arusha agreement and involving UNAMIR. Its missions: article 54

Apprehension:

- Collusion between the Belgian forces and the RPF
- Several rumors circulated
- Security of the country in general of the city of Kigali in particular

Stakeholders

- The UNAMIR
- The National Gendarmerie
- The Rwandan army
- The RPF (with the RPF battalion in legislation to come out)
- Private security companies
- ...
- Neighborhood watch organized by the civilian population

Mode of action

- Stationary and mobile controls
- Search and search by warrant
- Disassembly of weapon systems

Work to do

On the national territory

Offer the necessary facilities to UNAMIR in the spirit of the document on the agreement between the UN and the government of the Republic of Rwanda on the status of UNAMIR

To remember from this document
- Facilitate work at UNAMIR (Diplomatic Corps)
- Tamper-proof premises
- Attitude in the event of a violation (page 42)

On the national level
- Security rests with the government
- Rwandan Armed Forces must prepare a document

City of Kigali

Establishment of UNAMIR work teams in the camps

Measures and precautions to take

- Removing troops from sensitive locations
- Separate weapons and ammunitions

On the outskirts: arrangements in place

UNAMIR meeting at MINADEF on 12/27/1993

A. *Operation/security measures in the consignment area*
Need to standardize requests from UNAMIR teams

Possible demonstrations: not near the CND[7] intersections and surroundings

Informing the public

Individual weapons to soldiers living outside

What about transport for the Presidential Guard Camp?

Commission of Inquiry into Kabatwa and Kidaho Events: No government representation

Relocation of the Belgian contingent no later than January 3, 1994,

B. *Perspectives*
4-5 days ahead very critical

Operation clean corridor;

- Ensure strict security (consign soldiers rigorously)
- Significant presence of UNAMIR around the CND for the security of the CND - access by persons to be identified

---

7. Conseil National du Development or Rwandan National Assembly.

- Peripheral Guard
- Vehicle for transporting armed escorts

MINADEF, 1/07/1994

1. Preparation action by Inkotanyi for a probable attack on 1/08/1994
- Method
  - Prior Inkotanyi - FFR junction near the DMZ
  - Then attack in the city of Kigali
  - Friction
2. UNAMIR reaction (remove weapons from people)
3. Exit by RPF troops in uniform
4. Gendarmerie escort for cooperation, presidential guard reaction (Marchal at the wheel)
5. Grade sample
6. RPF: arms the population in DMZ
7. Escort: Rulindo

UNAMIR meeting at MINADEF on 01/12/1994

- UNAMIR's relationship with operational sector commands (all)
- Procedure for confiscating weapons
- Regulation of RPF battalion stay in Kigali
- Control of movements between the area occupied by the RPF and the Rwandan Army.
- Liaison officer?
- Reciprocal information
- Decrease in armed banditry
- Using Jali's Model Group
- Working with the population: neighborhood work teams
- Insufficient resources to fulfill all required missions

Debates

- Escorts problem: people to escort
- Carrying of individual weapons by officers: ok but concretely an authorization

Escort: supply vehicles, military, vehicles coming from the interior to Kigali, mayors carrying out missions

Reserve on military escorts moving within the Kigali area.

Hy Armament; no ammunition next to the pieces. What about Mount Kigali?

Armored Weaponry: Gather in a depot. Helicopter: disassemble.

MINADEF, 01/19/1994 (MINADEF-UNAMIR)

Agenda

1. Joint Mixed Commission
- Challenges ahead
- Should we wait for the establishment of institutions?

Designation of working groups

Meeting: January 27, 1994, in Ngondore tentatively, UNAMIR-RPF contact, levels of representation to be determined by UNAMIR.

2. Reconnaissance plan
G3 Gendarmerie and Army Command with UNAMIR planning officers

3. Carrying of arms
- In the weapons storage area: list of authorities to be escorted
- Weapons carried illegally
- The joint operation: list of people who regularly hold weapons (personalities who specifically claim the protection of UNAMIR. Sample weapon permits. What about UNAMIR's role in the custody of private dignitaries

1. List of military personalities to be escorted: work had already been done to determine the identification measures.
2. Mode of information to the population: to be done by UNAMIR and MINADEF to avoid misinformation
3. Patrol base

RPF movement control

- Entry and exit of RPF people. Impact of this information: tension in the population

- Issuance of identification cards for RPF soldiers
- Control of weapons to avoid any disappearance in Kigali
- Control of loading and unloading

Co-location of headquarters (QG)

- UNOMUR[8]: Kabale (Uganda)
- UNAMIR: UNAMIR Observation HQ in Mulindi, HQ in Ruhengeri, Byumba, Sector HQ in Kigali, HQ in Butare for Southern Sector
- Mutara
- Establishment of the transitional government
- Search for illegally held weapons; develop a concept

Meeting in Ngondore

Comments on the document

Establishment of the various points should take into general account considerations to be agreed between the two parties

This question arose in particular in the past when the Group of Neutral Military Observers (GOMN) tried to create a demarcation zone between the belligerents by offering the RPF, and the Rwandan government forces a simultaneous and equal retreat on the ground.

A buffer zone exists, and the locations occupied by the various forces are well known to UNAMIR, to which operational helmets have been transmitted.

What is the meaning of the new demarcation line proposed by UNAMIR, and in its view, what attitude should the opposing forces face after establishing this line?

Then explain the principles by page and paragraph

---

8. The United Nations Observer Mission Uganda–Rwanda (UNOMUR) was a peacekeeping mission established by the United Nations Security Council in Resolution 846 and lasted from June 1993 to September 1994.

Ruhengeri – Gatuma Axis

- Study on the Gatuna-Byumba axis at the request of the Rwandan president. My question: how about the Ruhengeri – Cyanika, Kanyonza – Kagitumba corridors?
- Importance of opening the three corridors on all the remote passageways that do not require repair work.

Two solutions

- Contingent
- Mutation

Issues Raised

- Difficult integration in Burundi
- J D Bu: Doc Uniform

Ruhengeri operational sector visit by MINADEF: 1/08/1994

A word from the sector commander

- Times are hard
- Dialogue between higher and lower ranks
- Kigali city influence is inevitable
- Influence of the Kigali—base axis (action too visible + attitudes)
- Infiltration Corridor
- Deep Demilitarized Zone

Enemy situation ahead

- A bit like from a device point of view
- Reconnaissance activity up to Mumba
- Many infiltrators
- Finding difficult information
- Treatment of accomplices?
- Attitude to intercepted vehicles?

State of mind of our soldiers

Factors adverse to morale

- Current political situation
- Tomorrow's uncertainty
- Demobilization operation plus integration (the officer section is even concerned since the appointment of student second lieutenants)
- Difficult logistics (outfits)
- Housing shortage
- Status problem: promotion whose effects are no longer perceptible, especially between the 22nd and 27th promotion. Unlike the young promoted and the old, these promotions have won nothing. What about the advancement of the promotion of technical officers?
- Too much mobility in fractions
- Discipline: more or less good under all these factors

Relations with the civilian population

- Cases of killings of civilians and soldiers that have tarnished civil-military relations
- Very little cooperation from civilians, not even an invitation from the civil authorities

Arms theft

20 weapons have been stolen so far since December 1993

Many sensitization meetings but in vain; the penalties are not dissuasive (payment of the weapon, termination of contract)

=> **Solutions**

1. Weapon detectors?
2. Lock the military in prisons
3. Sell the objects that the military have

Study the problem in anticipation of the resumption of hostilities!!!

MINADEF's intervention

- Infiltration: permeable sector. The extent of the infiltrators certainly, but rumors too.
- Deterioration of civil-military relations
- Collaboration with administrative authorities
- Arms theft. Destination: Burundi, banditry
- Military records/ state of mind

Debate

A. *Infiltrations*
- Information in the sector and demilitarized zones
- Collaboration with the population, especially at this time
- Revitalize surveillance at the barriers
- Base Zone Control

Information fees
- Provoke civil-military collaboration
- Detective training

Relations with the population

Weapon theft: intervention ok but difficult legal procedures

Mindset:
- Apoliticism
- demobilizations: 476 officers concerned => wait for the preparation of the files

Logistics: (commissioning problem)
- Ten thousand outfits to order

Accommodation
- Will become more complicated following the presence of UNAMIR
- Travel, especially at weddings; status to refine

Promotion (corporals)
- Rebalance advancement conditions
- Plan the military career of officers
- Technical officers: 20 technicians + Dr. Ntamuhanga and Kazenga

Instability in function
- At least 2 years old - war difficulty - rotation - location of losses - swapping: ok

MINADEF meeting with the troops

Raising Individual Issues/Questions by Support:

On promotions, on authorizations to marry within 3 years instead of 5, on the possibility of receiving a non-commissioned officer's card after 4 years, request for transfer, on the control of infiltrators through the vehicles of humanitarian organizations...

Other points raised: existence or not of the Medal of Honor? Promotion question? Remuneration, Logistics (outfits, boots, blankets), lack of medicines and medical care, demand for social change, putting pressure on politicians who do not want to end the war? Ready, for the safety of military families under attack?

Visit of MINADEF to the operational sector of Byumba

Presentation by the commander of the operational sector of Byumba: +- 6000 soldiers; proximity to the enemy

A. G1 Topics[9]
- Insufficient supervision
- The concern of officers following the lack of promotion commission
- Advancement plan benefit under Arusha:
- Officers from promotions ranging from 22 to 27
- Advancement of Majors not accounting for delays
- Cancellation of penalties before integration
- Many senior officers compared to the number of places
- Organization of the population during the resumption of hostilities (popular self-defense should not come under the sector command alone)

---

9. G stands for General Staff. It indicates offices on the headquarters, where G1 corresponds to G1 personnel, manning, admin, G2 intelligence, security, G3 Operations, G4 Logistics.

B. *G2 Topics*
- Moral problem related to:
- Frequently missing (safety of funds)
- Outfits: last distribution at the beginning of 1992 of at least one complete outfit per man plus blanket
- Lack of intelligence on the enemy in the demilitarized zones due to a lack of means
- Ambiguous political situation (last meeting of the parties today)

The Inkotanyi in Kigali: more than 600 people
- UNAMIR liaison officer is ill; therefore, to be replaced
- UNAMIR or RPF movements not reported.
- Hard time; uncertainty following the current situation

C. *G3 Topics*
- Organization of the instruction: difficult to make too large a distribution - population density
- Liaison problem at the battalion level following the resumption of non-replaced PPRs (talks) and the lack of plausible liaison between the army staff and the operational command.
- Operation: coordinate with Mutara

D. *G4 Topics*
- Habitations
- Equipment
- Charrois (more or less 40 immobilized vehicles - credit the 6000000; fuels: reduce social travel)
- Organization of autonomous supply in 48 hours: two days of ammunition combat at sector level; it takes saving within 48 hours.

Intervention by MINADEF
- The shape of the coming war
  - The war will be generalized, hence the resistance of the population - reflection MINADEF/UNAMIR
  - Mentoring - make an effort: posting plan for officers being at UNR (National University of Rwanda) + requisition plan
- Army cohesion to be highlighted, information of a political nature by MINADEF

- To remember
  - MINADEF's promise to provide one uniform per man to the Byumba operational sector command
  - Reflect on popular self-defense
  - Plan: Assignment of UNR Officers / Requisition
  - Reflect on the organization of instruction
  - Set up rewards and allowances
  - Rapid implementation of reinstated officers, otherwise revision of the act of integration
  - Propose a liaison officer to replace Lieutenant-Colonel Ndekezi
- Thanks
  - To the Minister for the time granted and response to the military
  - It is up to the operational sector to work with bravery: be vigilant in the face of RPF manipulations and enemies too close
  - Encourage people (Implementation of the Minister's guidelines; reflection on the form of war from which preparation => plans for survival, self-defense to be refined; requisition plan)
  - Arms theft: apply the measures
  - Money Theft: Security of Funds

Meeting with the troops

- Thanks to the Minister for a visit and for holding
- Individual grievances: Regularizing grades; request for social and individual transfers, 13th month, the double military specialty (secretary-accountants not considered while driver-mechanic; what about?)

MINADEF visit to the operational sector of the city

Mission: Defense of Kigali on two perimeters

Other difficulties:

- G1 topics (Regularization of seniority of officers, etc.)
- G2 topics: concrete attitude towards the infiltrators! Insufficient information due to lack of means)
- G3 topics: battalion stretch and supply issues; a battalion of Huye commandos cut in half; deployment of the UNAMIR

reduced the Elm (elements) Rwandan defense on sensitive points.

- G4 topics: difficult supply, insufficient ammunition, old and insufficient cartage.

Speech by MINADEF

- His joy to be within the Cyg (Cyangugu) battalion, which knew him as Prefect (Provincial governor)
- Socioeconomic situation of the country
  - Famine
  - Deficit of 16 billion Rwandan francs and the balance of payments
  - Reward employees
  - A large number of bandits => source of insecurity
  - University unemployment in the countryside
  - Mortality rate following illness, malnutrition
  - Burundian refugees
  - Hutu/Tutsi problem
- The political situation of the country
  - Reason for blockage in the establishment of transitional institutions
  - Consequences of the absence of the broad-based transitional government: (paralysis of the administration and mismanagement of political affairs)
- Military Situation - RPF
  - Willingness to fight?
    o Collaboration between (Uganda's) National Resistance Army (NRA) - FPR
    o The concentration of troops and equipment on the ground
    o Intensification of enemy reconnaissance
    o Presence of fighters disguised as soldiers
    o The current campaign of intoxication
    o Arms theft
    o Imitation of ranks by the Interahamwe
    o Outings in civilians anonymous
  - RPF strengths
    o Political Chaos in Rwanda

- o Tougher disciplinary system
- o Indoctrination of troops
- Weakness
  - o Accommodation
  - o Lassitude
- Behavior of our soldiers
  - Idleness resulting in serious indiscipline
  - rms theft
- Special case of the city operating sector: gun theft, bad relations, party influence
- Demobilization psychosis
- Collaboration army-population (to favor, and organize the population, arms theft)
- Issue link
- Remarks people:
  - Cinema internship: what about the certificate
  - Non-distribution of support funds
  - Mutual system
  - Why not exclude the Liberal Party (before forming the government)
  - Psychosis of demobilization
  - Theft of money (In addition to the safe; pay the money to the public treasury. To be planned in the meeting: salary payment system and security of funds)

MINADEF visit to Mutara operational sector - 02/16/1994

Interview with the troops

- Word from the Operational Sector Commander:
  - Incident in Muvumba commune
  - Five murders in Nyagatare
  - Bad climate: between those who come from Tanzania and those who dispute land and between leaders and people
  - Relations between the military and the population
  - Reduced wrongdoing
  - Morale: influencing factors

- G1 Domain
  - Promotion of staff cadets with influence on seniority
  - Advancement of Technical Officers
  - Seniority of officers who became major
  - Fate of officers who have not completed their training
  - Broad-based transitional government will end the remaining problem in the army
  - Members who want to rotate
- G2 Domain
  - Refugees returned to Shonga = intervention with international organizations
  - Map of the region
- G3 Domain
  - little radio
  - Quote for work
- G4 Domain
  - Clothing and equipment - boots
  - Equipment of reintegrated soldiers
  - Purchase of jerry cans
- Individual grievances
  - Specialists having never been in the field
  - Members who have lost their card
  - Support funds
  - Lack of logistics
  - Remuneration for leave; regularization of wages, ...
  - Request for transfers
  - Supply Difficulty
  - Disease problems, etc.
- Intervention of the Chief of Staff
  - Thank the Minister and encourage him
  - Thank Mutara military, but think of avoiding idleness and correcting mistakes made in war; to question ourselves. Regarding rotations: agreement for inter-sector rotations. Seniority: Corporal Dispatch Started
  - Poverty problem
  - Estimated quote for weapons
  - Money for leave: studied

MINADEF meeting on 02/17/1994

Coordination of plans

Current enemy situation:

- More or less 20,000 men (battle line, elite battalions, infiltrators)
- Strengths: support from Uganda, the establishment of infiltrators, political chaos, unpunished action
- Weakness: demystification, vulnerability; line of communication, logistics: the population, population alerted by Europeans and international opinion

Enemy Possibilities

Junction after a long infiltration => action in town. Fixing on the entire front and opening other fronts

Justification

- Political blockage
- Accentuate the chaos

G3 (staff officer) presentation

Quaternary organization

At the tactical level

Entrenched position

Reserve at the level of each battalion and ???

At the general level,

Battalions held in reserve: special forces (para-commando), reconnaissance, Huye, and Gitarama

Intervention of the staff of the national gendarmerie

Participation of the gendarmerie in combat actions

- The Tutsis will be brought to safety => decisive attention
- Attention from the camps => Turn of G3 + return of the soldiers to the units

- Attitude of UNAMIR
- Actions to be taken at the diplomatic level
- Can they win and take over?

G3 Domain

- Rotation of soldiers in position
- Permutation of the PL (platoon) PM (Military Police)
- Determine the objectives of the training (executive troop)

G4 Domain

- Liquidation of salaries: enact measures to avoid theft of military pay
- Cartage issue: G4 battalion and Gitarama battalion
- Outfits and boots
- Transportation costs and drug purchases
- The problem of fuel and food shortages
- Insufficient ammo issue

Speech by General Déogratias Nsabimana on the occasion of his appointment to the rank of Officer of the National Order of the (French) Legion of Honor

Allocution général Nsabimana

Allocution prononcée par le général major Nsabimana Déogratias, à l'occasion de sa nomination au rang d'officier de l'Ordre National de la Légion d'honneur.

Excellence Monsieur le Ministre de la Défense,

Excellence monsieur l'Ambassadeur,

General Nsabimana's speech

Speech delivered by Major General Nsabimana Déogratias, on the occasion of his appointment to the rank of Officer of the National Order of the (French) Legion of Honor.

Your Excellency the Minister of Defence,

Excellency Ambassador,

Mesdames, Messieurs

Chers amis,

Je n'aurais pas besoin, je pense, d'insister sur l'émotion qui m'étreint aujourd'hui: elle est assez visible je crois, beaucoup plus en tout cas que je ne le voudrais.

Car on a beau dire et beau faire, lorsqu'on se trouve ainsi reconnu par l'élite d'une grande nation comme la France, on ne peut s'empêcher de se dire qu'on a peut-être eu raison, de mener sa vie comme on l'a fait.

Ladies and gentlemen
Dear friends,

I don't think I need to emphasize the feeling that holds me today: it's fairly obvious, I suppose, much more than I'd like.

All told, it is impossible not to believe that we may have been right, in leading our lives as we did, when we find ourselves recognized in this way by the elite of a great nation like France.

Excellence Monsieur l'Ambassadeur,

Je suis très honorée par la distinction qui m'a été conférée, et à laquelle je n'avais jamais aspiré. En effet, dans mes actions, dans mes décisions ou à mon travail quotidien, je n'ai songé à aucun moment à cette récompense suprême destinée, depuis le règne de l'Empereur Napoléon Bonaparte aux éminentes personnalités françaises aussi bien civiles que militaires.

Excellency Mr. Ambassador,

It is an honor for me to be granted this distinction, which I had never aspired to. Indeed, in my actions, in my decisions or in my daily work, I never thought at any time of this supreme reward intended, since the reign of Emperor Napoleon Bonaparte, for eminent French personalities, both civilian and military.

N'étant pas de nationalité française, c'est pour moi une fois de plus l'occasion d'être fier de ce mérite, et de rendre un juste hommage aux autorités françaises — représentées par vous-même Excellence Monsieur l'Ambassadeur — qui ont daigné me décerner cette distinction, au-delà de tous préjugés.

Mais j'ai aussi mille raisons de m'interroger sur les mérites ainsi reconnus. Qu'ai-je fait pour la France ou tout simplement pour les Français résidant au Rwanda?

Despite the fact that I am not of French nationality, this is another reason for me to be proud of this distinction and to give a proper appreciation to the French authorities —represented by yourself, Excellency Mr Ambassador — who deigned to bestow this honor on me.

But I have a thousand reasons to doubt the qualities so acknowledged. What have I done for France, or merely for the French in Rwanda?

Si je devais bénéficier de ce mérite, c'est grâce à vous Excellence Monsieur l'Ambassadeur, et sûrement, grâce aux membres de la Mission d'Assistance Militaire française au Rwanda et, aux camarades de l'armée française, qui sont toujours restés à mes côtés pendant cette période de trouble que traverse notre pays. Que tout cela trouve ici l'expression de ma profonde gratitude. Mon éloquence n'étant pas suffisante pour traduire ce sentiment à leur égard, c'est bien simplement, bien franchement, bien sincèrement que je leur adresse un grand merci, tout en vous priant Excellence, d'être mon interprète auprès des plus hautes autorités françaises pour leur transmettre mes sentiments d'un hommage déférent. Que cette récompense serve une fois de plus, à renforcer les liens d'amitié existant entre les peuples français et rwandais et plus particulièrement, entre l'armée française et l'armée rwandaise.

If I were to benefit from this merit, it is thanks to your Excellency Mr. Ambassador, and certainly, thanks to the members of the French Military Assistance Mission in Rwanda and to the comrades of the French army, who have always remained by my side during this period of trouble that our country is going through. May all this find here the expression of my deep gratitude. I lack the eloquence to translate this feeling towards them, it is very simply, very frankly, very sincerely that I send them a heartfelt thank you, while pleading with you, Excellency, to act as my interpreter with the highest French authorities in order to transmit my emotions of reverent regards. May this reward serve once again to strengthen the bonds of friendship between the French and Rwandan peoples and more particularly, between the French army and the Rwandan army.

Monsieur le Ministre,
Monsieur l'Ambassadeur,
Mesdames, Messieurs,
Chers amis,

La question sur les mérites, je me la pose également pour le Rwanda: ai-je bien servi mon pays ? Il ne m'appartient pas de le dire, mais je m'y suis toujours efforcé. Non pas en ma qualité d'officier, mais tout simplement comme tout autre citoyen, militaire ou civil, mû par l'idéal de servir sa patrie.

**Minister,
Mr. Ambassador,
Ladies and gentlemen,
Dear friends,**

In terms of merit, I also ask myself for Rwanda, «Have I served my country well?» It is not for me to say, but I have always tried, not as an

officer, but as any other citizen, military or civilian, motivated by the concept of service to country.

Je suis convaincu que si sa mission et néanmoins et moi théorique et moins spectaculaire que celle d'un soldat au combat, le civil lui-aussi, dans l'ombre feutrée d'un bureau, ou dans l'exercice quotidien d'un métier ordinaire, peut grandement contribuer au prestige de sa nation.

Excellence monsieur l'Ambassadeur,

Cette distinction que vous me décernez aujourd'hui, permettez-moi de la partager moralement avec tous ceux qui, dans des moments difficiles que je n'ai pas voulu évoquer, m'ont compris, aidé et encouragé. Car son prestige est-elle, que je crois bien de ne pas le mériter seul.

Civilians, despite their less dramatic and theoretical missions than soldiers in combat, can also greatly contribute to the prestige of their nation, even in the hushed shadow of an office or in the daily exercise of an ordinary profession.

Honorable Ambassador,

Allow me to share this honor, which you are bestowing upon me today, morally with all those who, during tough periods that I will not specify, understood, assisted, and encouraged me. Because of its prestige, which I believe is well deserved.

Acknowledgements

From the bottom of my heart to all those who have contributed directly or indirectly to the production of this book:

To Mom for her unwavering love and for pushing us to publish this book.

To our companions and children for their moral support and for having endured our moods and tensions in this long and difficult undertaking.

To Lieutenant-Colonel Maurin and the late Major Gijsbrechts for organizing our evacuation to safety.

To the Kyembwa and Mugengararo-Uwizeyimana families for offering us shelter during the first months of our lives as refugees.

To Ambassador Johan Swinnen for writing the Preface and James R. Doty, M.D., for writing the Afterword for ou book.

To Charles Onana: you were the first to publicly express your compassion for us as victims. May your tireless struggle for the exposing of truth be heard.

To Cathy Cherrak, for your proofreading and your corrections in keeping with the spirit of the story.

To Alex Dumba for your invaluable artistic assistance.

To anyone who reads this book.

Finally, a big thank you to my brothers and sisters, Maurice, Denise, Yvonne, Josiane, and Fabrice: we are stronger together.

MIX
Paper
FSC® C100212

Printed by Imprimerie Gauvin
Gatineau, Québec